UNNATURAL
AFFECTIONS

Unnatural Affections

The Impuritan Ethic of Homosexuality and the Modern Church

George Grant and Mark Horne

LEGACY
COMMUNICATIONS

Legacy Press
A Division of Legacy Communications
P.O. Box 680365
Franklin, Tennessee 37068-0365

To Our Wives
Karen and Jennifer
Whose Natural Affections
Sustain Us Always

Y Gwyr Erbyn Byd

CONTENTS

ACKNOWLEDGEMENTS

E very book—even one as small as this one—is the result of the thinking, encouragement, and diligence of many people. And of course, this book is no exception.

When a special task force appointed by the Presbyterian Church, United States of America, released a controversial report on Christian sexuality, entitled, *Keeping Body and Soul Together: Sexuality, Spirituality, and Social Justice,* the entire Christian community was shocked. Believers—across all denominational lines—were thrown into the midst of a crisis. Thankfully, in God's good providence, a group of concerned men and women quickly emerged demonstrating to a watching world an unwavering Christ-like faithfulness. Great thanks go to that group—the Presbyterian Lay Committee—for staying the course and for sharing our enthusiasm for this project.

In addition, David Dunham, Steve Diggs, and Jack Watts all afforded us with their love, their wisdom, their patience, their good humor, and their technical support. Peter Leithart and David Chilton gave unselfishly of their time, energy, and expertise. Similarly, our co-workers, Nancy Britt, Mary Jane Morris, Luc Nadeau, Jim Small, and Charles Wolfe stood by us even when we were rather cranky due to sleep deprivation and writers' panic. To all these friends, we offer our sincerest gratitude.

But it is to our wives, Karen and Jennifer, that we owe our deepest debt. No thanks could ever be enough for all that they do and all that they are (Philippians 1:3–11).

Feast of Michael and the Angels
Fort Lauderdale, Florida

They exchanged their natural affections for that which is entirely unnatural. They burned in their desire for one another, women with women and men with men, committing indecent acts and receiving in their own persons the due penalty of their error.

(Romans 1:27–28)

INTRODUCTION:
LANCE'S STORY

horresco referens [1]

"Beyond our greatest pleasures there lie dangers." [2]

G.K. Chesterton

I n ancient Greece, the festival of Bacchus was held each
year to celebrate the spring harvest. It was always a cha-
otic and raucous affair. During the obstreperous week-long
festivities, the normally sedate city states of the Pelopenese
succumbed to animal passions and compulsive caprices.
They profligately indulged in every form of sensual gratifi-
cation imaginable—from fornication and sodomy to intoxi-
cation and gluttony. It was an orgy of promiscuous
pleasure.

Bacchus was the god of wine, sex, and song. To the
Greeks, he was the epitome of pleasure. His mythic exploits
were a dominant theme in the popular art, music, and
ideas of the day. Chroniclers of the age tell us that the
annual carnival—called the bacchanal—commemorating
his legend was actually the bawdy highlight of the year. In
fact, it dominated the Hellenic calendar then even more
than Christmastide does ours today.

But a wild picture of immorality which only poets and
mobs can understand is always simultaneously a wild pic-

1

ture of melancholy which only parents and emissaries can understand. Thus, even as they revelled in the streets, the ancients were troubled by a sublime sadness. It was like an ache in their throats or a knot in their stomachs, but it was actually an abscess in their souls. Even as they celebrated their gay gaiety, they were forced to acknowledge their human unhappiness.

Ultimately, it was the bacchanal's smothering culture of sexual excess that proved to be the undoing of Greek dominance in the world. Historians from Thucydides and Heroditus to Himmelfarb and Schlossberg have documented that the social collapse of Hellenism was rooted in the moral collapse of Hellenism. The reason is as simple as it is universal.

Just as liberty and equality are opposite extremes often contrary to freedom, so sensuality and satisfaction are opposite extremes often contrary to happiness. There is, in fact, no real connection between the pursuit of happiness and the pursuit of pleasure. Happiness and pleasure are indeed, in a sense, antithetical things, since happiness is founded on the value of something eternal while pleasure is founded on the value of something ephemeral.

Sadly, the lessons of history are all too often lost on those who most need to learn them.

The first time I ever witnessed a "Gay Pride Parade," I was astonished—and I was reminded instantly of those ancient bacchanals. The raucous revelry, the perverse promiscuity, the orgiastic opulence, and the appolyonic abandon that I saw in the Montrose section of Houston seemed almost identical to the descriptions I had read of the Greeks on the precipice of their demise. The malevolent scene before me could have easily been transported three thousand miles and three thousand years to the bustling Plaka under the shadow of the Acropolis without missing a beat. The sights and sounds would have been no more alien there than here.

It was on that disorienting day in that discordant place that I first encountered the despondent distress of homosexuality—it was there and then that I first met Lance.

We were as opposite as night and day. He was an exuberant participant in the day's festivities—cavorting in the aura of libertine excess. I was a member of an evangelistic team—inviting people to attend a Bible study that I conducted for those who were interested in deliverance from the captivity of that same libertine excess. He was cocky, idealistic, and tragically self-sure. I was nervous, gloomy, and profoundly self-conscious. He was only just recently "out of the closet." I was only just recently married. He was appalled by my mission. I was no less alarmed by his.

Ironically, we became quick friends.

Paradox is at the root of all true friendships. The tensions of likes and dislikes, similarities and differences, comparisons and contrasts must be delicately balanced for mere comradery to mature into genuine openness. And so our odd relationship grew in fits and starts.

He periodically attended our Bible study, but always left infuriated. Marshalling tattered, second-hand arguments from wishful-thinking-liberals and salon-chair-expositors, he railed against the very plain teaching of Scripture on the subject of sexuality in general and homosexuality in particular. He first tried the tired tack of assailing Biblical authority. Failing at that, he tried some creative exegetical gymnastics. In desperation he attacked particularly onerous episodes in Church history or obviously noxious inconsistencies in Church practice. His torturous logical contortions became convincing evidence that all too often, a man's theology is shaped by his morality—not the other way around. He simply would not give up a fancy under the shock of a fact.

Even so, Lance seriously sought for a substantive justification for his sexual orientation and practice. His unhappiness was gnawing at mind, body, and spirit. He yearned for something more than what the saturnalias of the gay bars offered. He yearned for something more than what the bacchanalias of the gay parades offered. Laboring night and day like a factory, he poured through every scrap of literature he could find on the subject—both what I gave him and what he could dredge up on his own.

"I had become desperate," he told me sometime later. "I knew that I was so lost I didn't know which way was up. I was so lonely—and the anonymous sex I had at the bars and bath houses only intensified that loneliness. The only place that I found any kind of authenticity was at the Bible study. But that grated on me terribly. I can remember sitting outside your apartment in my car debating whether or not I should go in. I felt damned if I did and damned if I didn't. Now I know that I was simply under conviction, but at the time I just knew that I was miserable."

For a few months, he tried to assuage his anguish by going to the services of a local pro-homosexual congregation. "I thought that might relieve the pressure I was feeling," he explained. "But it only made things worse. The inconsistency of that kind of pick-and-choose Christianity was obvious to me right away. I determined that I had only two choices: accept Christianity as a whole or reject it as a whole. The option of winnowing out the parts I liked and trashing the rest—cafeteria-style—just seemed like the height of hypocrisy."

Indeed, hypocrisy is the tribute that error pays to truth, and inconsistency is the tribute that iniquity renders to integrity.

For several years Lance struggled with the enigmas of grace and truth. He watched as several of his former friends and lovers were alternately rescued by the Gospel or consumed by AIDS. Meanwhile, the downward spiral of his promiscuity accelerated alarmingly.

There were times when he would cut off all contact with me—for months on end. Then he would show up at my door for desperation counseling. Finally, late one Friday night, he yielded and trusted Christ for the very first time.

"There was no instant flash of revelation," he said. "No fireworks. No bells and whistles. I had just come to the end of myself."

But a profound change began to occur in his life nonetheless—a change that continues to evidence itself even to this day.

I have been privileged to see God similarly at work in the lives of innumerable homosexual men and women through the years. That is why I have never shared the fear that many Christians have of the "gay liberation movement." I have personally witnessed real liberation too many times. Spiritual longing is the soft underbelly of the modern homosexual bacchanalia. Even militant groups like Act Up, Queer Nation, Wham, and Wisk don't seem to me to be a significant challenge to the Gospel.

But there is one threat that I am very concerned about—if successful, it could stymie any efforts to reach people like Lance with the message of hope and truth. That threat is a compromised Church.

And thus this small book.

Growing out of tense and terse apprehension—that the tidal wave of accommodation of many mainline Protestant denominations might actually engulf the Church life and mission—this introduction to the subject was compiled so that congregations might have the background necessary to make wise decisions. So that individuals might have the courage to stand against the tide.

It is offered under the assumption that whatever is right is actually good, that whatever is good is actually just, and that whatever is just is actually merciful. The kindest and most compassionate message that Christians can convey to homosexuals and their defenders is an unwaveringly Biblical message.

The structure of this book is thus quite simple and straightforward:

Chapter One surveys the current crisis in the Church—focusing particularly on the drift of the mainline Methodist, Episcopal, and Presbyterian denominations into a treacherous kind of latitudinarianism.

Chapter Two examines how the world has effectively influenced the Church—rather than the other way around—on the question of homosexuality.

Chapter Three looks at the issue of authority—specifically the relevance of the Bible to the formulation of our sexual doctrines and dogmas.

Chapter Four attempts to encapsulate the legacy of twenty centuries of Church tradition and teaching on homosexual practices.

And finally, Chapter Five is a practical summary with a series of applications necessary to restore our culture to sanity and justice.

Conspicuous by their absence are any arguments rooted in sociological quandaries. There is a simple reason for that: homosexuality is not problematic because it is politically obnoxious, or culturally offensive, or socially subversive, or organizationally anarchic, or emotionally destructive, or personally selfish, or medically pathogenic. Rather, it is problematic because the "faith once and for all delivered to the saints" says that it is problematic. Period. All those other concerns, though actually very real, are but incidentally symptomatic.

So you won't find here a lot of detailed descriptions about the destructiveness of the gay lifestyle or long diatribes about the necessity of AIDS testing. Instead, you will find a plea to the Church to simply do what it is supposed to do—and be what it is supposed to be.

Deo soli gloria. Jesu juva.[3]

1

THE CRACK IN
THE CATHEDRAL

corpus delicti [1]

"The pessimist can be enraged at evil. But only the optimist can be surprised at it." [2]

G.K. Chesterton

John and Linda Ahlstrom were utterly astonished. They had just heard that a committee designated by their denomination to reexamine the Church's stand on sexual morality had abandoned traditional and Scriptural values. Instead, it had embraced the prevailing morality of the surrounding culture—affirming the compatibility of premarital sex, extramarital sex, and homosexuality with Christian faith and practice.

"Who would have ever dreamed that these kinds of behaviors would one day be condoned by the Church?" John asked incredulously. "By the world, sure. By a few fringe groups, maybe. But by the Church? No way. I've been a Presbyterian all my life. My parents and grandparents were faithful members of the Church before me. Through the years, I've seen a lot of crazy things. But this beats all."

"I'm not really sure why they even want to call what they believe *Christian* any more," added Linda. "Just where is the line of distinction between faith and faithlessness? If a Church ceases to believe Christian doctrine, if it denies Christian tradition, if it rejects Christian values, and if it denounces Christian behavior, can we continue to legitimately call it *Christian?* I have to admit: I have my doubts."

"We're supposed to be the place where the world turns for answers to the toughest questions in life," said John. "But instead, we've turned that completely backwards. Here we are in the midst of some of the most difficult days ever, and the Church almost appears to be in worse shape than even the world."

"It seems to me that the Church has walked out on a limb this time," Linda agreed. "It is really in trouble."

This Present Crisis

Indeed, the modern Church is in trouble. Real trouble.

Though its attendance is growing, its influence is diminishing. Though its giving is up, its impact is down. Though its profile is heightened, its vitality is lessened. And that is not even the worst of it. The Church today is divided against itself—locked into a fierce conflict over the most basic questions of ethics and morality.

"I am more worried about the Evangelical faith in this country than ever," says author and pastor Michael Scott Horton. "I wonder if Evangelical Christianity can survive another era of being tossed back and forth with every wind and doctrine."[3]

And he is not alone. Recently, innumerable voices have joined together in a chorus of concern:

Theologian R. C. Sproul characterizes the Church as, "continuing to slide into the morass of theological relativism and subjectivism."[4] Renowned social commentator Charles Colson refers to American Christianity as, "a Church in exile."[5] Church historian Martin Marty laments that, "the Church today may be in more difficulty and travail than at any other time in its long history. Scandals on every side, divisions, schisms, conflicts, avarice, and simple greed have very nearly made the Church a laughingstock."[6] The newly installed Archbishop of Canterbury, George Carey confides, "I fear for the future. The Church seems to have lost its way."[7] Evangelist Billy Graham concurred, saying, "I'm not certain what the future holds for the institutional Church, but at the moment it looks grim." Presbyterian leader D. James Kennedy argues that, "there is little hope for the world if the Church cannot agree on the simplest of things—like what is right and what is wrong." And the respected leader of mainstream Evangelical renewal during the last three decades, the late Francis Schaeffer, evaluated the state of the American Church in our day as "the great Evangelical disaster."[8]

Without a doubt, the Church is in trouble. Or rather, with a great *many* doubts the Church is in trouble. Doubts are becoming all the Church is known for raising. Not doctrinal truth. Not the level of debate. And certainly not the dead. Just doubts. For the Church—which is supposed to be the discipler of the nations (Matthew 28:19), the ruler of the world (Matthew 16:19; Revelation 20:4), and "the pillar and ground of the truth" (1 Timothy 3:15)—no longer proclaims a common confession, but speaks with a "scattered voice."[9] Every day seems to bring headlines of new ethical scandals, divisions over doctrine, and revisions of revelation. Many of the long-accepted verities of the Christian faith are being rejected for the vagaries of the contemporary consensus of confusion.

Though this crisis in the Church directly affects many modern issues, perhaps the most visible and certainly the most volatile is the debate over the Church's teaching on and treatment of homosexuals. The fact is the division within the visible Church over homosexuality is representative of almost all that is troubling Christianity today. It inescapably involves the issue of Biblical authority, the nature of Church ministry, the scope of Church discipline, and the Church's responsibility and relationship to the civil sphere.

War in Heaven

Skirmishes and full-fledged battles in this civil war of values seem to constantly break out within the Church. Three recent major denominational struggles especially demonstrate the crisis facing the modern Church.

The United Methodist Church, for instance, has been torn asunder by a controversy over traditional Christian sexual morality. In 1988, a proposal was brought before the denomination's General Conference to remove from the Church's long-standing official statement of social principles that homosexual orientation or practice is "incompatible with Christian teaching." After three years of debate, eighteen members of a twenty-four-member panel released a report calling for the elimination of the traditional statement on homosexuality. Four other members released a dissenting report calling for the statement to remain. The two remaining refused to sign either report.

Both sides agreed that there is disagreement among medical and sociological "experts" over the "causes" of homosexuality. Both agreed that the Church must urge the recognition and protection of "basic rights and civil liberties" of homosexuals. Both agreed that the Church should be a place of acceptance for homosexuals—after all, United Methodists already practice some level of acceptance because two of the members of the study committee were themselves self-professing homosexuals. The only substantial difference between the two reports was that the majority claimed current scientific, philosophical, and theological knowledge "does not provide a satisfactory basis upon which the Church can responsibly maintain the condemnation of all homosexual practice," while the minority claimed that same current lack of expert consensus "does not provide a satisfactory basis upon which the Church can responsibly alter its previously held position."

Both reports have been met with the ire of rank-and-file Methodists. Should either be sent to the next General Conference, a firestorm of controversy is sure to erupt. Opposing battlements are already in place.

When a recent straw poll showed that the committee favored codifying the majority report, the denominational office was deluged with mail—almost ninety-five percent of which supported the Church's traditional stand that homosexuality is entirely incompatible with Christian teaching. Additionally, thirty-five of fifty regional conferences debating the issue of homosexual practice rejected any ethical exemptions for homosexuality.[10] Conservatives have been optimistic about their chances of maintaining a clear Biblical affirmation of sexual morality. James Heidinger, executive secretary of Good News, a conservative caucus within the Methodist Church, contends that "we have indicators from annual conferences that we will see the strongest Evangelical delegation going to General Conference that we have seen in thirty to fifty years."[11]

However, liberal groups are also preparing for the upcoming General Conference. A special interest group within the denomination, the Methodist Federation for Social Action, has resolved to ask delegates at the Conference to remove any prohibitions of the ordination of homosexuals. Another group, Affirmation, recently changed their name to reflect the heightened tensions. The group is now called Affirmation: United Methodists for Lesbian, Gay, and Bisexual Concerns.[12]

Whatever the ultimate outcome, this conflict over basic sexual morality has already taken its toll. The Church lost more than sixty thousand members last year alone. And since 1968, the once powerful Church has shrunk from eleven million members to under nine million.[13]

Sadly, this modern crisis of creedal identity has not been limited to the United Methodists. The Episcopal

Church is also reeling from internal division over the issue of homosexuality.

At their July 1991 triennial convention, the Episcopalian leadership was unable to resolve the debate over homosexuality. While on the one hand a resolution was passed "affirming the teaching of the Episcopal Church that physical sexual expression is appropriate only within life-long monogamous marriage," on the other hand, the resolution claimed there is "discontinuity" between this teaching "and the experience of many members of this body."[14] Conservatives proposed canon law requiring clergy to abstain from all unbiblical sex, while liberals tried to pass a measure affirming homosexual practice and allowing the ordination of gays. Both attempts failed.[15]

This "discontinuity" effectively destroyed all attempts to enforce the "teaching of the Episcopal Church." The proposed censure of two bishops for ordaining non-celibate homosexuals as a violation of the Church's 1979 resolution which declared such ordinations "not appropriate," was refused in favor of a declaration that they had caused "pain and damage to the credibility of this house and to parts of the whole Church."[16] In light of the fact that many bishops openly admitted ordaining homosexuals and some priests gave public testimony about their homosexual practices, the failure of the Church to censure its errant clergy established a debilitating precedent—essentially, Episcopal bishops can simply do as they please.

Seven hundred sixty-five Episcopal Church members at the triennial convention, who were mostly from the Evangelical, charismatic, and Anglo-Catholic wings of the fragmenting denomination, signed a "statement of conscience" protesting the unwillingness of the Church to take a stand.[17] In addition, the conservative Episcopal Synod of America, which claims two hundred chapters throughout the Church, declared that Episcopalians were divided into "two religions," and further stated: "A Church which affirms Biblical truths but cannot discipline those who reject

them has descended to the level of any ot¹
tution and thus cannot win the world for u.
One conservative wrote, "Both sides recognize the)
tronized by an amorphous, cowardly center that idoliz⌐
false sense of unity."[19]

And so the battle rages.

Presbyterians—like the Methodists and the Episcopalians—are also fractiously divided over the issue of homosexuality and sexual fidelity. Recently, a special task force on human sexuality appointed by the mainstream Presbyterian Church, United States of America, produced a startling report that has garnered tremendous interest nationwide. Because it completely rejects twenty centuries of Christian consensus on sexual mores, the report has been more than a little controversial. Most of the national media reported that the report—entitled, *Keeping Body and Soul Together: Sexuality, Spirituality, and Social Justice*—was rejected by the General Assembly of the denomination. Actually though, the delegates merely instructed another committee to construct a plan to present at the next annual Assembly, "to assist the Church in exploring significant Biblical, theological, and ethical issues raised in the Church around human sexuality during this past year," and told them to use the controversial report as one of their resources along with a dissenting minority report and other denominational pronouncements.[20]

The General Assembly also voted to send a pastoral letter to all their congregations assuring members that "we have affirmed in no uncertain terms the authority of the Old and New Testaments" and have "strongly reaffirmed the sanctity of the marriage covenant between one man and one woman to be a God-given relationship to be honored by marital fidelity."[21]

In fact, an attempt to affirm that monogamous marriage is "the only God-ordained relationship for the expression of sexual intercourse" was rejected in favor of simply stating that marriage was "a God-given relationship" for sexual intercourse.[22]

Both sides of the tortured debate were frustrated by the General Assembly's decision. Homosexuals want to know why they cannot be ordained if they are welcome in the Church. And others wonder, if homosexuality is a sin which keeps practitioners from being ordained, why are they not subject to Church discipline?[23]

According to Elisabet Hannon of Presbyterians for Gay and Lesbian Concerns:

> Every proposed action that would have represented progress to gay and lesbian people failed. But so did every proposed action that would have made us more fundamentalistic on sexuality. At least, individuals will have access to this very important document. I think we can claim a victory in that.[24]

The disputed document was two-hundred pages long with forty-eight recommendations. It advocated: reversing the long-standing prohibition of homosexual ordination; developing "resources" for "recognition" of same-sex relationships; and requesting the denominational Board of Pensions to change its programs to allow same-sex couples to receive medical and retirement benefits.[25]

The document was written by the Task Force on Human Sexuality which had drawn criticism from its inception some five years ago. Critics have argued that the group's membership was not at all representative of the Church at large. Indeed, a poll found that ninety percent of mainline Presbyterians oppose the ordination of homosexuals, as do ninety-five percent of ruling elders and lay officers.[26]

Sadly, additional examples abound. The Christian Church—or the Disciples of Christ—is another denomination losing members over the issue of homosexuality.[27] The United Church of Canada's recent sharp decline in membership can be attributed to their decision to make the ordination of practicing homosexuals possible.[28] The size of the National Council of Churches may soon be reduced by a fourth because Eastern Orthodox communions may leave in protest over the acceptance of homosexuality by member communions as well as the Council's dialogue with the Metropolitan Community Church, an almost exclusively homosexual denomination.[29] The bottom line is that, with very few exceptions, the issue of homosexuality is tearing the Church apart.

The Court Prophets

Laboring night and day like factories, the forces advocating the complete abandonment of traditional values have raised up several key spokesmen—who by virtue of their prominence and influence have successfully dominated the debate thus far.

Probably the loudest and most tenacious advocate of homosexual orientation and practice in the Church is the Episcopal Bishop of Newark, John Shelby Spong. Though his best known book is *Rescuing the Bible from Fundamentalism: A Bishop Rethinks the Meaning of Scripture*,[30]—an unabashed Humanist tract which radically recasts the whole content of Scripture—his previous work was *Living in Sin: A Bishop Rethinks Human Sexuality*,[31] written to justify the acceptance of homosexuals by the Church. Spong gained national notoriety when he defied Church standards and ordained a homosexual priest, Robert Williams, who later embarrassed the bishop by publicly blasting monogamy.[32] Nevertheless, at the triennial conference of the Episcopal Church, Bishop Spong announced he would soon ordain another gay priest.[33]

A more Evangelical voice calling for Christians to rethink their attitudes toward homosexuals is Tony Campolo, a professor of Sociology at Eastern College, an ordained Baptist minister, and a popular speaker. Campolo argues that not all people with "homosexual orientations" are "perverting their original nature." At a meeting of the Evangelical Round Table he stated:

> Paul, in Romans 1, condemned one *kind* of homosexual behavior which is a perversion resulting from an insatiable sexual appetite yielded to the demonic.[34]

Campolo went on to suggest that homosexual lovers ought to live together in a lifelong covenant without having sex. He explained:

> There are Christians who might disapprove of this arrangement, claiming that the Bible implies a condemnation of even romantic feelings between members of the same sex. However, these critics are hard-pressed to build a Biblical case for their complaints.[35]

Spong and Campolo have had a tremendous impact on the shape and tenor of the debate over sexual ethics in general and homosexuality in general. That is clear enough. What is astonishing is that more and more people—people who claim to believe and follow the Bible as the sole standard for faith and practice—are calling on Christians to reconsider the attitude of the Church toward homosexuality. Such a revolution does not bode well for the future of the faith. It does not bode well in the least.

Conclusion

The Church is supposed to stand united. Jesus' last prayer was that His disciples "might be one." Unity is absolutely essential for the Church's witness to the world. Our unity actually demonstrates to unbelievers that God sent Jesus into the world (John 17:20). A Church publicly at odds over any issue is a terrible contradiction that sends a mixed message to the world. But a Church divided against itself over such basic ethical standards is an unconscionable tragedy.

Even so, Christ did not pray for unity at any cost. He prayed that His people be kept in truth: "Sanctify them by Your truth. Your word is truth" (John 17:17). He prayed that truth might be a means of protecting his disciples from becoming merely part "of the world." After all, the Church is supposed to be *in* the world, not *of* it.

To pursue unity at the expense of truth is an exercise in futility. To compromise the truth does not lead to unity with the Church, but to unity with the world.

"I hate all the squabbling and fighting," John Ahlstrom said. "But I hate the complete abandonment of our faith—which was once and for all delivered to the saints—even more. At some point you just have to take a stand."

"And we're taking our stand here," his wife Linda asserted. "For the sake of our Church, for the sake of our children, and for the sake of the future of our civilization. Right here. On the truth. That is where we'll stand."

2

THE STORM AT SEA

ab aeterno [1]

"The hardest thing to remember about our own time is simply that it is a time." [2]

G.K. Chesterton

A nn Hacklander said she felt like she "was in China, not in the United States." The Wisconsin woman had just been subjected to a four-and-a-half hour session with the Madison Equal Opportunities Commission. Ann was found guilty of a housing-code violation because she turned down a lesbian she interviewed to become her roommate because she was uncomfortable at the thought of living with a homosexual. Ann was ordered to pay five hundred dollars to the offended lesbian, attend sensitivity-training classes conducted by a homosexual rights group, and submit to monitoring by the commission for two years to make sure her attitude improved.

For what it's worth, the lease was in her name. [3]

Judy Allison, an apartment manager in Atlanta, is being sued for various civil rights and housing violations as well as discrimination against the handicapped. Her crime? She told an AIDS-infected man who exhibited the disease's characteristic skin lesions to get out of the apartment complex's swimming pool. Tenant Jerrod Beasley, who had

19

invited the man to the complex, phoned the Lambda Legal Defense Fund and initiated the legal action. In response to Allison's concern for other swimmers, including a pregnant woman, Beasley stated that "everyone knows" AIDS is not transmissible from a swimming pool. But what he failed to mention was that even if catching the Human Immunodeficiency Virus is not a problem, AIDS-infected people, because of their very low resistance to germs and infection, commonly carry a host of other diseases that could easily spread in a swimming pool.

Allison can be prosecuted for discrimination against the handicapped because the Americans With Disabilities Act, which President George Bush signed into law, defines people with the deadly disease as "handicapped."[4]

Many may wonder: How have we come to this?

Traditional Immorality

In ancient societies, there was nothing resembling the Christian sexual ideal of heterosexual monogamy. Fertility cults involving temple prostitution and orgies, both heterosexual and homosexual, were actually quite commonplace. According to historian Peter Leithart, ancient paganism naturally gave rise to such sexual practices. He says that this was simply because:

> It was essentially a worship of nature, and the practice of ritual sex was rooted in this naturalistic worldview. In ancient mythology, in which we can see distortions of the Genesis account, order emerged from chaos . . . In the chaos and fertility cults man participates in divine life and recovers fertility by a ritual reenactment of the original act of a myth, often of the creation from chaos. Ritual chaos, in short, recreates, reorders, and reanimates the world. Sexual orgies are one part of the ritual reenactment of chaos.[5]

Furthermore, in many of those post-deluvian societies, homosexual relationships were encouraged as a positive good. This is most notably true in the case of the ancient Greeks. Sodomy was not only practiced, but held up as a philosophical ideal. According to Leithart, "Plato's most poetic hymns on love grew out of reflections on pederasty."[6] In fact, Socrates argued that promiscuous homosexuality was a superior form of love because it united "the love of a beautiful body" with "the love of a beautiful soul"—something he believed was rarely accomplished through chaste heterosexuality.[7]

Dennis Prager, a contemporary Jewish scholar contrasts Old Testament Israel with these surrounding pagan societies:

> Except for the introduction of a universal, moral, supernatural God, nothing was as radically different, as unnatural, and as anti-social as its prohibition of homosexuality . . . Man-boy love has been an accepted, even lauded feature of most civilizations. It dominated Greece, and has been an accepted norm in the Arab and Muslim world until the present century. Sir Richard Burton reported that the Chinese love of homosexuality was only equaled by their love of bestiality.[8]

The lesson of history is indisputable: apart from those cultures guided and directed by the Bible, human society has never maintained what most American Christians regard as traditional family values. Only the gradual missionary expansion—and ultimately the cultural dominance—of Christianity can explain the existence of the sexual ethic which we today consider natural.

The Return to Tradition

From the sixteenth century onward, the Christian ethic of chaste fidelity began to be undermined first by the Renaissance—due to the exaltation of the pagan Greek classics—and then further by the Enlightenment. For more than a millennium the Church had maintained that any and all sexual activity outside the sacred bond of marriage was sinful—thus, for instance, it thought homosexuals were responsible for their behavior and that their behavior was immoral—but the new secular movements kept looking back to the old pagan promiscuity. Again according to Leithart:

> In the final analysis, as one would expect, the Enlightenment rejection of Christian sexual morality led to a justification of all sexual perversions. In an important sense, Western Enlightenment sexual ethics were far more perverse than their pre-Christian models, for they were self-consciously rejecting Christianity, and like the dog that returns to his vomit, were in the last condition worse than the first (2 Peter 2:22). We are still living with the consequences of the Enlightenment's triumph over Christianity.[9]

This triumph, involved the acceptance of three central tenets which were directly contrary to the confession of the Christian Church:

First, the Enlightenment encouraged a virtual worship of nature. The natural environment was the standard against which moral behavior was to be measured. This of course necessitated a rejection of the Bible as the ethical foundation of culture. Nature became, according to historian Carl Becker, "the new revelation."[10]

Second, because nature was considered normative, and humanity was viewed as a mere product of nature, anything people did "naturally" in thought, word, or deed was considered normal or even good. In other words, these modern secular movements denied the existence of original sin. By Renaissance and Enlightenment standards, only that which suppressed what men did naturally could be considered evil.

Third, this environmental Humanism ultimately led to a kind of insipid primitivism—an obsession with "the virtues of either distant primitive civilizations, or of the distant, and more virtuous past of European civilization itself."[11] After all, if nature is good, then the closer people are to nature the better they will be. Since the primitive peoples commonly had perverse sexual customs, the new humanistic thinkers used them as evidence that Christian morality must be an artificial aberration. The typical example of this kind of theorization is found in the writings of Jean-Jacques Rousseau, who asserted that monogamy was an artificial contrivance exploited by women to "establish their empire."[12]

Despite their best efforts at propounding these anti-Christian notions, for at least two centuries the Humanists were profoundly unsuccessful in debunking the solid Christian consensus in the West. But their relentless assault on morality continued anyway. Many Humanists believed it was simply a matter of time before their sensual predilections would prevail.

The Making of Modernism

Following the Enlightenment, non-Christian thought continued to develop in direct opposition to the sexual ethic of the Church—going so far as to assert a radical rejection of personal responsibility for sexual, or any other kind of behavior.

So for instance, the romantic philosopher and atheist, Friedrich Nietzsche—anticipating much of contemporary psychology—explained the expansive humanist position on morality in his typically candid style:

> Today we no longer have any pity for the concept of "free will": we know only too well what it really is—the foulest of all theologians' artifices, aimed at making mankind "responsible." . . . Wherever responsibilities are sought, it is usually the instinct of wanting to judge and punish which is at work. The doctrine of the will has been invented essentially for the purpose of punishment, that is, because one wanted to impute guilt. The entire

that is, because one wanted to impute guilt. The entire old psychology, the psychology of will, was conditioned by the fact that its originators, the priests at the head of ancient communities, wanted for themselves the right to punish—or wanted to create for themselves the right to punish—so that they might become *guilty:* consequently, every act had to be considered as willed, and the origin of every act had to be considered as lying within the consciousness . . . Christianity is a metaphysics of the hangman.[13]

Of course, most of the Church's opponents were not as honest about their intentions at first. They did not attempt to openly contradict Christian teaching, as much as subtly work to undermine its foundations. Societal norms which had long been based on the Christian world-and-life view, were not necessarily altered but offered a new "more scientific" basis.

This "bait and switch" tactic was successfully accomplished primarily through the discipline of psychology—especially the work of Sigmund Freud. Freud invented a bizarre Darwinian explanation for sexual behavior which "medicalized" sex and said that homosexuality "is assuredly no advantage, but it is nothing to be ashamed of, no vice, no degradation."[14]

Thus, according to one philosopher:

Freud's achievement was to make sex a medical, rather than a moral problem, a biological issue of sickness and cure rather than sin and redemption . . . Freud attempted to help people adjust to their perversions so that they could live productively, happily. and efficiently while continuing to spit on God's commandments.[15]

Homosexuality, though still considered aberrant, was no longer called a sin, but a sickness. Until as recently as 1970, the American Psychiatric Association's official publication, the *Diagnostic and Statistical Manual of Psychiatric Disorders,* listed homosexuality as a mental illness.[16]

From Disease to Dignity

By the beginning of this century, modern psychology, sociology, and anthropology—having substituted science for Scripture as the authoritative basis for sexual morality—had secured their cultural tenure enough to actually attack the Christian ethic directly. To a great degree this dramatic shift was the direct result of the work of Alfred Kinsey. In his 1948 *Report on Male Sexuality* he made many shocking claims, one of which was that thirty-seven percent of American men had at least one homosexual experience between adolescence and old age. The popular scientific acceptance of Kinsey's findings profoundly undermined the generally accepted Christian notions that homosexuality is a deviant behavior.

Kinsey asserted that all forms of copulation—whether heterosexual, homosexual, or other—were equal. All that mattered was the mechanical achievement of an orgasm. How it was achieved was irrelevant. Since Kinsey's data showed that "everyone was doing it," he was able to make a convincing case that our society's ethical norms should be revised to match our society's actual practices. Homosexuality began to gain acceptance as a normal alternative lifestyle. Recently, new evidence has demonstrated that Kinsey's work was actually fraudulent and unscientific—besides being in violation of laws against the sexual molestation of children. Even so, the damage is done.[17]

Kinsey's conclusions ultimately found their way into the practice of therapeutic medical care. The American Psychiatric Association, for instance, removed homosexuality from its list of abnormal behaviors and mental illnesses. It did so not because it had made some new scientific discoveries or had found compelling clinical documentation of Kinsey's thesis. Rather, it simply capitulated to direct pressure.

The American Psychiatric Association ceased to define homosexuality as a mental illness simply and solely because, beginning at the 1970 convention, homosexual activists launched an intense campaign involving disruption and intimidation to coerce doctors to change their diagnosis. Instead of standing their ground, the leaders of the association tried to placate the homosexuals with concessions. By 1973, the homosexuals gained enough clout to completely alter the long-standing designation. Ronald Bayer, in his *Homosexuality and American Psychiatry*[18]—which is actually very sympathetic to the homosexual lobby—is surprisingly forthright about their methods in confronting the psychiatric profession:

> There was a shift in the role of demonstrations from a form of expression to a tactic of disruption. In this regard gay activists mirrored the passage of a confrontation politics that had become the cutting edge of radical and antiwar student groups. The purpose of the protest was no longer to make public a point of view, but rather to halt unacceptable activities. With ideology seen as an instrument of domination, the traditional willingness to tolerate the views of one's opponents was discarded.[19]

Since that time homosexuals have continued to effectively use demonstrations and tactics of disruption to gain their agenda. They have not only lobbied for the repeal of state and local anti-sodomy laws, but have worked to lower the age of consent across the board.[20]

Legislating Immorality

But the homosexual agenda has involved much more than merely removing criminal penalties for their behavior. By demanding "civil rights" legislation, the homosexual lobby is forcing the government to actively endorse their behavior through the power of law. This is already happening in various cities, just ask Ann Hacklander. Under "civil rights" housing codes, it is becoming a crime for a Christian to refuse to rent an apartment to a homosexual.

Additionally, homosexuals have been frighteningly effective in gaining control of influential institutions—most notably the public schools. The National Gay and Lesbian Task Force, a lobbying group in the nation's capital, demands that sex education courses which present homosexuality as a "healthy alternative lifestyle," be taught by gays and lesbians.[21] Syndicated columnist Don Feder reports that the National Association for the Education of Young Children, the largest accreditation agency for preschool education, had the Gay and Lesbian Caucus make a presentation on "sexual preference, pride and the early childhood educator" at their 1990 conference.[22] In Miami, despite a statute mandating that schools teach "abstinence outside of marriage" and "the benefits of heterosexual marriage," the school board has officially approved a call-in phone line for children which in a recorded message tells them that homosexuals are "a non-ethnic, non-racial minority group." Furthermore, students who dial the automated call-in system are assured that "sexual orientation is not a choice. It's a given. It can be compared to being left-handed." The number to this "educational service" is given out by teachers to public school students, and the phone-line is partly sponsored by the Florida state government.

The Federal Government is also involved in promoting homosexuality. The Thirteenth National Lesbian and Gay Health Conference, for example, which took place in July of 1991, was supported with twenty-five thousand dollars from the Centers for Disease Control. Topics at the conference included "Creating Mythologies and Rituals for Queer People," "The Lesbian Erotic Dance," "Sexcessful Teen Outreach," and "Eroticizing Safer Sex for Women."[23] The National Endowment for the Arts, under the direction of Chairman John Frohnmayer, has funded one work of homosexual, sadomasochistic pornography after another. On July 16, 1991, the Public Broadcasting System aired "Tongues Untied," "an explicit film about the trials faced by black homosexual men," which was also funded by our tax dollars—as was the San Francisco International Gay and Lesbian Film Festival where the film was originally shown.[24]

Perhaps even more chilling is the virtual legal revolution that is taking place, in which the civil government is being empowered to punish people for what they think. President Bush signed the so-called "Hate Crimes Bill" into law—which is "the first legislative recognition of homosexuality at the federal level."[25] The law, which enables the government to keep track of crimes impelled by politically incorrect motives, lays the groundwork for additional and more punitive statutes in the days ahead. At the very least such laws create odd inequities in the system by giving certain fashionable minorities special privileges in criminal justice. So for instance, if a person was convicted of killing someone because he didn't like the "minority group" to which the victim belonged he would be punished more severely than if he had murdered for mere money, thrills, or personal animosity.[26]

Worse, the new "Hate Crimes" legislation would not only punish people for what they do, but for what they say—or even think. Florida legislators recently capitulated to the homosexual lobby and passed a law enhancing penalties for crimes "that evidence prejudice based on race, religion, ethnicity, color, ancestry, *sexual orientation,* or national origin." In addition, the law states that any "person or organization which establishes that it has been coerced, intimidated, or threatened shall have a civil cause of action for treble damages, an injunction or other appropriate relief in law or in equity." This could have an ominous effect on Churches that preach and teach the Biblical perspective—that homosexuality is actually sin. One attorney pointed out that the law "creates a completely subjective standard: anyone can prove that he or she was intimidated simply by swearing that was so."[27]

From Dignity to Disease

No discussion about our society's present crisis in sexual ethics could be complete without mentioning Acquired Immune Deficiency Syndrome—or AIDS. The message to the public on AIDS has been mind-bogglingly contradictory. So, on the one hand, we are told that "AIDS isn't a gay disease" since it is caused by a contagious virus that will infect anyone, whether or not he is homosexual. On the other hand, any attempt to quarantine those infected with the Human Immunodeficiency Virus—or HIV—has been condemned as somehow "homophobic"—as if treating AIDS like any other contagious, deadly disease is just a disguised attack on homosexuals.

While AIDS has not yet become the widespread epidemic it was predicted to be, it has been an effective tool for getting the homosexual agenda promulgated through public schools and elsewhere—all in the name of "health." It has also been used for its civil rights value. Through some torturous feat of twisted logic, the Americans with Disabilities Act defines people who appear to be AIDS-infected as legally "handicapped" and, therefore, protected from discrimination.

Conclusion

Nothing illustrates the tragedy of the world we live in better than the frightened letter a teenage boy wrote to an advice columnist about desires he was experiencing and did not like.

> You've got to help me! I am fifteen and I'm afraid I'm gay. I keep getting interested in guys. I don't even dare take showers after gym because I get aroused. I'm so scared. I don't want this. I try and try not to think this way, but I can't stop. I'm going to kill myself if there's no way to make me straight.

The columnist's reply was a model in "politically correct"
thinking:

> You can't change your fantasies, no matter how hard you
> try. You can control what you do about it, but not what
> you think. Don't consider suicide! Call a teen hotline
> and find someone who understands. Many gay teen-agers
> feel desperately lonely and isolated because they know
> they will be discriminated against and hounded if they
> come out. An alarming number do take their own
> lives.[28]

She went on to recommend a homosexual support
group.

There is no way of knowing if this anonymous boy was
able to see through the deceptive reply he received and
find help, or if he came to accept the message of modern
society: "You have no choice. You cannot help yourself. You
are not responsible. You must accept yourself the way you
are."

But this we do know: The radical transformation of our
society's sexual ethics has come in direct contradistinction
to the teaching of Scripture. And more, it is in direct contradistinction to the cultural standards that have made
Western Civilization what it is. Thus we appear to be treading on terribly treacherous turf.

3

THE FIRM FOUNDATION

ad limina apostolorum [1]

"The age of skepticism put caricature into ephemeral fenilleton; but the ages of faith built caricature into their Churches of everlasting stone." [2]

G.K. Chesterton

W hat is truth?" asked Pontius Pilate before he sent an innocent man to be tortured to death. Indeed, Pilate was very much a modern man. For his question lies unspoken behind the debate in the Church over homosexuality.

Jesus said, "I am the way, the truth, and the life" (John 14:6). While some may want to reduce the Lord's statement to mere mysticism, He meant much more than that. The fact that Jesus *is* the Truth means that He *speaks* the truth. Constantly throughout the Gospels, Jesus is recorded prefacing his teachings by saying, "Truly, truly, I say to you." He made clear to His hearers that His words were more enduring than all creation: "Heaven and earth will pass away, but my words will never pass away" (Luke 21:33).

Furthermore, Christ affirmed that even the books of the Old Testament were the Word of God and true in every way, shape, and form. He made it clear that "the Scripture cannot be broken" (John 10:34). He did not hesitate to appeal to the Word of God as an absolute standard for all behavior: "Why do you also transgress the commandment of God because of your traditions" (Matthew 15:3).

Jesus divided humanity into two classifications: Those who heard, believed, and obeyed His Word, and those who did not hear, disbelieved, and disobeyed His Word. Christians—that is, followers of Christ—are, *by definition*, those who respond obediently to His Word and are gathered into His Church (John 10:1-18).

Of course, Jesus did not simply write down His message directly, but spoke by His Spirit through His designated disciples, just as He had spoken through the Old Testament prophets. In the same way that He superintended the Old Testament work of Moses and the prophets, He superintended the work of the Apostles which has been providentially handed down to the Church in the form of the New Testament.

The bottom line is the Bible is the Word of God and true in all that it contains. This is an inescapable presupposition woven throughout all of the Scriptures:

- "Your righteousness is an everlasting righteousness, and Your law is truth." (Psalm 119:142)

- "The entirety of Your word is truth, And every one of Your righteous judgments endures forever." (Psalm 119:160)

- "And he who has seen has testified, and his testimony is true; and he knows that he is telling the truth, so that you may believe." (John 19:35)

- "These words are faithful and true." (Revelation 22:6)

But the Bible is not merely true, it is also useful, important, and necessary as guidance for daily living:

- "You shall therefore keep His statutes and His commandments which I command you today, that it may go well with you and with your children after you, and that you may prolong your days in the land which the LORD your God is giving you for all time." (Deuteronomy 4:40)

- "I have more understanding than all my teachers, for Your testimonies are my meditation." (Psalm 119:99)

- "All Scripture is given by inspiration of God, and is profitable for doctrine, for reproof, for correction, for instruction in righteousness, that the man of God may be complete, thoroughly equipped for every good work." (2 Timothy 3:16–17)

In addition, the Bible provides a check on our own waywardness and perversity. It convicts us of our sins in thought, word, and deed which—otherwise—we would not recognize as sin:

- "Your word I have hidden in my heart, that I might not sin against You." (Psalm 119:11)

- "There is a way that seems right to a man, But its end is the way of death." (Proverbs 14:12)

As Christians, all our opinions must be in line with the teachings of Scripture. As Christian philosopher Cornelius Van Til asserted:

The Bible is thought of as authoritative on everything of which it speaks. And it speaks of everything. We do not mean that it speaks of football games, of atoms, etc., directly, but we do mean that it speaks of everything either directly or indirectly. It tells us not only of the Christ and his work but it also tells us who God is and whence the universe has come. It gives us a philosophy of history as well as history. Moreover, the information on these subjects is woven into an inextricable whole. It is only if you reject the Bible as the Word of God that you can separate its so-called religious and moral instruction from what it says, e.g., about the physical universe.[3]

The Purpose of the Word

According to Jesus, we are to obey the precepts and statutes of God's Word *because* we have been justified. We do not obey them *in order to be* justified. Obedience to the Word is the *effect* of salvation, not the *cause* of salvation. In other words, the Scriptural fealty is designed to be a tool of sanctification, not the *means* of justification and redemption. It is a way of *life*, not a way of *salvation*.

Jesus constantly upheld the validity of God's Word as a guide for living and an expression of the unchanging standards of His rule:

- "Man shall not live on bread alone, but on every word that proceeds out of the mouth of God." (Matthew 4:4)

- "It is easier for heaven and earth to pass away than for one stroke of a letter of the Law to fail." (Luke 16:17)

- "Whoever then annuls one of the least of these commandments, and so teaches others, shall be called least in the Kingdom of Heaven; but whoever keeps and teaches them, he shall be called great in the Kingdom of Heaven." (Matthew 5:19)

Again and again He affirmed the truth that "All Scripture is God breathed" (2 Timothy 3:16), and that it "cannot be broken" (John 10:35). He did not come to do away with the Word—to abolish or abrogate it. On the contrary, He came to fulfill it—to confirm and uphold it (Matthew 5:17). He reiterated the fact that every one of "His righteous ordinances is everlasting" (Psalm 119:160) and that "the Word of our God shall stand forever" (Isaiah 40:8).

Jesus was affirming that, unlike human lawmakers, God does not change His mind or alter His standards: "My covenant I will not violate, nor will I alter the utterance of My lips" (Psalm 89:34). When the Lord speaks, His Word stands firm forever. His assessments of right and wrong do not change from age to age: "All His precepts are trustworthy.

They are established forever and ever, to be performed with faithfulness and uprightness" (Psalm 111:7–8).

Jesus appealed to Old Testament statutes to bolster His teaching (John 8:17). He used them to vindicate His behavior (Matthew 12:5). He used them to answer His questioners (Luke 10:26), to indict His opponents (John 7:19), to identify God's will (Matthew 19:17), to establish Kingdom citizenship (Matthew 7:24), to confront Satan (Matthew 4:1–11), and to confirm Christian love (John 14:21). He was, in short, a champion of the Word.

But He also put the Old Testament in its place. He showed us that the commandments are not designed to effect *salvation* for men. Instead, they are designed to effect *sanctification* for men. They are designed to enable men to submit to and evidence the rule of God.

This is what the Apostle Paul meant when he said that we are no longer "under the Law" (Romans 6:14–15), that in fact we are "dead to the Law" (Romans 7:4; Galatians 2:19). Instead, we are under the sacrificial covering of Christ's blood fulfilling the death sentence of the law against us (Romans 8:1–2). But Law is not made void; its curse is (Galatians 3:13). In fact, when the Law is put in its proper place, it is "established" (Romans 3:31).

The Bible is the Word of God. It is His revelation of wisdom, knowledge, understanding, and truth. It is not simply a splendid collection of inspiring sayings and stories. It is God's message to man. It is God's instruction. It is God's direction. It is God's guideline, His plumb line, and His bottom line.

Thus, as Christians it is absolutely essential that we take every single aspect of God's Word to us very seriously—and then attempt to live under its authority in every detail of our lives.

Beginning at the Beginning

So what does the Bible teach about homosexuality? Whenever Jesus addressed issues of human sexuality, He used the original creation of man as a point of reference. The creation account demonstrates the importance of human sexuality: "So God created man in His own image; in the image of God He created Him; male and female He created them" (Genesis 1:27). Interestingly, the creation of both sexes is treated as essential for humanity to bear "the image of God." But notice, after God created the first man, Adam, He decided that he needed a companion:

> And the LORD God said, "it is not good that man should be alone; I will make him a helper comparable to him . . . And then the LORD God caused a deep sleep to fall on Adam, and he slept; and He took one of his ribs, and closed up the flesh in its place. Then the rib which the LORD God had taken from man He made into a woman, and He brought her to the man. And Adam said:
>
> "This is now bone of my bones and flesh of my flesh; She shall be called Woman, because she was taken out of Man."
>
> Therefore a man shall leave his father and mother and be joined to his wife, and they shall become one flesh.

Theologian Greg Bahnsen sums up the teaching of this Genesis account eloquently:

> This creation of sexual differentiation by God from the beginning established heterosexuality as the normative direction for the sexual impulse and act. God the Creator gives created things their essential identity and function and define's man's proper relationships. Man's sexual function has been defined by God as male-female behavior.[4]

The Ten Commandments

God spoke from Mt. Sinai in a thunderous voice, "You shall not commit adultery" (Exodus 20:14; Deuteronomy 5:18).

Thus he prohibited all sex outside of the holy bounds of marriage.

This standard was elaborated in the various case laws He gave Moses—laws which applied the Ten Commandments to specific issues in the life of God's people. For instance, "You shall not lie with a male as with a woman. It is an abomination" (Leviticus 18:22).

Strong words. In fact, this kind of covenantal violation is so serious in God's eyes that he declared it subject to a maximum penalty of capital punishment:

> If a man lies with a male as he lies with a woman, both of them have committed an abomination. They shall surely be put to death. Their blood shall be upon them. (Leviticus 20:13)

Through the years, many have tried to avoid the obvious significance of such passages. They have argued, for example, that such case-laws were only intended for the nation of Israel, and thus, have no additional application whatsoever. God clearly indicates, however, that other nations are judged by God for violating these laws. In fact, God told the Hebrews that He was annihilating the Canaanites for just such offenses.

> And you shall not walk in the statutes of the nation which I am casting out before you; for they commit all these things, and therefore I abhor them. (Leviticus 21:23)

Indeed, once the Hebrews had settled in the land, God told them that they were to be a witness to the nations around them which would be attracted by their laws. Plainly, God's prohibition of homosexuality applies to all peoples because God is the creator and sustainer of all of them and His Word is eternal—it "will by no means pass away" (Matthew 24:35).

God's condemnation of same-sex perversions is absolute and categorical—even homosexual partners who may be "committed and faithful" fall under His immutable bar of justice. There is no hint in Scripture that there are exceptions or aberrations to this standard—thus in the case laws, whereas any form of extramarital sex was a capital offense, pre-marital heterosexual offenses were adjudicated with an option of covenantal marriage (Exodus 22:16–17; Deuteronomy 22:28–29).

Even apart from the case laws, God's blanket condemnation of homosexuality is evident in numerable passages throughout Scripture—not the least of which is the story of His destruction of Sodom and Gomorrah. Though the cities were judged for several sins, rampant unchecked homosexuality ensured their fate (Ezekiel 16:49–50). According to Scripture, the divine judgment poured out on the cities was meant to be "an example to those who afterward would live ungodly" (2 Peter 2:6). Later, almost the entire Hebrew tribe of Benjamin was wiped out for behaving like Sodom. Still later, whenever the prophets of the Old Testament accused Israel of severe apostasy they would compare the nation to the city of Sodom (Isaiah 3:9; Jeremiah 23:14).

The Gospel

Many today would contend that there is a vast gulf of differentiation between the harsh teaching of the Old Testament and the fresh forgiveness of the New Testament—particularly when it comes to the issue of homosexuality. Jesus, for instance, is silent on the question, they would say. But that is simply not the case.

Though it is true that we have no record of Christ confronting or ministering to a known practicing homosexual, His message clearly prohibits any such behavior. For one thing, Jesus endorsed the teachings and commandments of the entire Old Testament. He never had any hesitation about that. He said that "heaven and earth would pass away" before the statutes of the Word passed away. Secondly, Jesus appealed directly to the creation account of one man and one woman as the sole model for covenant marriage. And like the Old Testament Prophets, Jesus used the example of Sodom's sin as a warning to Israel of divine wrath. Finally, Jesus made it clear to His disciples that the only option for those who do not marry, is celibacy (Matthew 19:11–12).

As Christianity moved out of Israel into the surrounding promiscuous and perverse pagan culture, the Apostles were forced to deal more directly with the issue of homosexuality. In Romans, Paul, under the superintendence of the Holy Spirit, condemns homosexuality as he discusses the consequences of suppressing God's revelation in creation:

> For this reason God gave them up to vile passions. For even their women exchanged the natural use for what is against nature. Likewise also the men, leaving the natural use of the woman, burned in their lust for one another, men with men committing what is shameful, and receiving in themselves the penalty of their error which was due. (Romans 1:26–27)

And, furthermore, writes the Apostle, "knowing the righteous judgment of God, that those who practice such things are worthy of death," they nevertheless, "not only do the same but also approve of those who practice them" (Romans 1:32). Notice here that the Scriptures condemn not only homosexual acts but homosexual desires. This principle is simply an application to homosexuality of what Jesus said about lust during the Sermon on the Mount:

> You have heard that it was said to those of old, "You shall not commit adultery." But I say to you that whoever looks at a woman to lust after her has already committed adultery with her in his heart. (Matthew 5:27–28)

Indeed, the Bible assumes that, contrary to popular opinion, men and women are responsible for their desires

and are capable of controlling them (Job 31:1,9; Proverbs
6:25).

Again and again throughout the New Testament, homosexuality is listed among those unacceptable sins of the
flesh from which the Gospel has liberated us:

- "Do not be deceived. Neither fornicators, nor idolaters,
  nor adulterers, nor homosexuals, nor sodomites, nor
  thieves, nor covetous, nor drunkards nor revilers, nor
  extortioners will inherit the kingdom of God." (1 Corinthians 6:9–10)

- "But we know the law is good if one uses it lawfully,
  knowing this: that the law is not made for a righteous
  person, but for the lawless and insubordinate, for the
  ungodly and for sinners, for the unholy and profane,
  for murderers of fathers and murderers of mothers, for
  manslayers, for fornicators, for sodomites, for kidnap-
  pers, for liars, for perjurers, and if there is any other
  thing that is contrary to sound doctrine, according to
  the glorious gospel of the blessed God which was committed to my trust." (1 Timothy 1:8–11)

Conclusion

The whole testimony of Scripture, from the beginning of
the Old Testament record, through the Gospels, and on to
the end of the New Testament is absolutely clear: homosexuality is sin whether committed in thought, word, or deed.
Further, God holds homosexuals responsible for their sin,
just as He does any other practicing sinner. Despite the
dogmatic insistence of those who believe that human be-
ings are either biologically or behaviorally determined,
Christians must insist that we have control over our "sexual
orientation." As Christian counselor Jay Adams has stated:

> One is not a homosexual constitutionally any more than
> one is an adulterer constitutionally. Homosexuality is not
> considered to be a condition, but an act. It is viewed as a
> sinful practice which can become a way of life. The ho-

mosexual act, like the act of adultery, is the reason for calling one a homosexual (of course one may commit homosexual sins of the heart, just as one may commit adultery in his heart. He may lust after a man in his heart as another may lust after a woman).[5]

Greg Bahnsen further explains:

Of course homosexuality may not be a conscious and remembered choice any more than is heterosexuality. There may not have been a process of explicit deliberation, weighing the options, and coming to a decision in either case. But that does not make homosexuality or heterosexuality any less chosen, in the sense of a voluntary, willful and personal preference. The occasional homosexual defense, "I can't help it," cannot be acceptable in light of the Word of God.[6]

The Gospel's message of the sinfulness of homosexuality has been reviled by some as an awful bigotry. It has been equated with the evils of racism—which are categorically condemned in Scripture. But the reality is that treating homosexuality as a sin is the very opposite of bigotry. For instead of simply stereotyping homosexuals as predetermined products of either their biology or environment, the Gospel treats them the same as every other sinner who needs to repent and believe. As author David Chilton writes:

Calling homosexuality a sin will seem to be a cruel, insensitive attitude, a "homophobic response" of condemnation rather than concern. But the truth is that it is the beginning of true freedom and joy for the homosexual. For if homosexuality were either an inescapable human condition (like height and skin color) or an incurable disease, there would be no hope. The homosexual would be locked in his lusts forever, with no possibility of escape. Once we see clearly that homosexuality is a sin, we can also see the way of deliverance.[7]

This is the message of the Gospel: Christ died for sinners—to set them free from sin. The Apostle Paul knew this well. After listing homosexuality among other sinful practices which exclude people from the Kingdom of God, he wrote to the Church in Corinth:

> And such were some of you. But you were washed, but you were sanctified, but you were justified in the name of the Lord Jesus and by the Spirit of our God. (1 Corinthians 6:11)

The New Testament Church, apparently, was filled with repentant ex-homosexuals who had found new life in Christ. May it be so once again.

4

THE TRUE TRADITION

artes moriendi [1]

"True tradition is exactly like a sonnet; it is a symbol of the soul." [2]

G.K. Chesterton

Winston Churchill once said that, "The greatest advances in human civilization have come when we recovered what we had lost: when we learned the lessons of history."[3] Sadly, that is a lesson lost on many—if not most—of our contemporaries.

One mark of the modern mind is an abrasive arrogance which assumes the past is useless in dealing with the pressing problems of the present. Worse, some Christians, caught like their unregenerate neighbors in a malignant contemporaneity, actually think that their disdain for the historic Christian traditions is pleasing to God. Indeed, many think that the purpose of the Protestant Reformation was to overthrow the Christian traditions.

It is, of course, true that we must obey God rather than men. We must not be like the Pharisees, "teaching as doctrines the commandments of men" (Mark 7:7; Isaiah 29:13). Indeed, one of the cries of the Reformation was *Sola Scriptura*—"Scripture alone!"

43

But this by no means nullifies the value of the traditions of the Church for the modern Christian. As Reformed theologian, James Jordan has written:

> The Bible teaches that tradition is important, because it
> is the heritage of the Spirit. The Spirit has raised up
> apostles, prophets, evangelists, and pastors/teachers, as
> well as other gifted persons. These persons are the gift of
> the Spirit. (The gifts of the Spirit are not abstract quali-
> ties, but gifted persons.) We despise the Spirit if we do
> not pay attention to the person-gifts He has given in the
> past, who formed the traditions of the Church.[4]

History is not just the concern of historians and social
scientists. It is not the lonely domain of political prognosti-
cators and ivory tower academics. It is the very stuff of life.
And, it is the very stuff of faith. In fact, the Bible puts a
heavy emphasis on historical awareness—not at all surpris-
ing considering the fact that the vast proportion of its own
contents record the dealings of God with men and nations
throughout the ages.

Again and again in the Scriptures, God calls upon His
people to *remember*. He calls on us to remember the bondage, oppression, and deliverance of Egypt (Exodus 13:3;
Deuteronomy 6:20–23). He calls on us to remember the
splendor, strength, and devotion of the Davidic Kingdom
(1 Chronicles 16:8–36). He calls on us to remember the
valor, forthrightness, and holiness of the prophets (James
5:7–11). He calls on us to remember the glories of creation
(Psalm 104:1–30), the devastation of the flood (2 Peter
2:4–11), the judgment of the great apostasies (Jude 5–11),
the miraculous events of the exodus (Deuteronomy 5:15),
the anguish of the desert wanderings (Deuteronomy 8:1–6),
the grief of the Babylonian exile (Psalm 137:1–6), the responsibility of the restoration (Ezra 9:5–15), the sanctity of
the Lord's Day (Exodus 20:8), the graciousness of the commandments (Numbers 15:39–40), and the ultimate victory
of the cross (1 Corinthians 11:23–26). He calls on us to

remember the lives and witness of all those who have gone before us in faith—forefathers, fathers, patriarchs, prophets, apostles, preachers, evangelists, martyrs, confessors, ascetics, and every righteous spirit made pure in Christ (1 Corinthians 10:1–11; Hebrews 11:3–40).

He calls on us to *remember*. As the Psalmist has said:

> We must remember the deeds of the Lord in our midst. Surely, we must remember His wonders of old. I will meditate on all Your work, and muse on Your deeds. Your way is holy; what god is like unto our God? You are the God who works wonders; You have made known Your strength among the peoples. You have by power redeemed Your people, the sons of Jacob and Joseph. (Psalm 77:11–15)

And again:

> Oh give thanks to the Lord, call upon His name. Make known His deeds among the peoples. Sing to Him, sing praises to Him; speak of all His wonders on the earth. Glory in His name; let the heart of those who seek the Lord be glad. Seek the Lord and His strength; seek His face continually. Remember His wonders which He has done in our midst, His marvels and the judgments uttered by His mouth. (Psalm 105:1–5)

When Moses stood before the Israelites at the end of his long life, he did not exhort them with polemics or moralisms. He reminded them of the works of God in history. He reminded them of their duty to *remember* (Deuteronomy 32:1–43).

When David stood before his family and friends following a great deliverance from his enemies, he did not stir them with sentiment or nostalgia. He reminded them of the works of God in history in a psalm of praise. He reminded them of their duty to *remember* (2 Samuel 22:1–51).

When Solomon stood before his subjects at the dedication of the newly constructed temple, he did not challenge them with logic or rhetoric. He simply reminded them of the works of God in history in a hymn of wisdom. He reminded them of their duty to *remember* (1 Kings 8:15–61).

When Nehemiah stood before the families of Jerusalem at the consecration of the rebuilt city walls, he did not bombard them with theology or theatrics. He simply reminded them of the works of God in history in a song of the covenant. He reminded them of their duty to *remember* (Nehemiah 9:9–38).

When Stephen stood before an accusing and enraged Sanhedrin, he did not confront them with apology or condemnation. He simply reminded them of the works of God in history in a litany of faith. He reminded them of their duty to *remember* (Acts 7:2–53).

Remembrance and forgetfulness are the measuring rods of faithfulness throughout the entire canon of Scripture. A family that passes its legacy on to its children will bear great fruit (Deuteronomy 8:2–10). A family that fails to take its heritage seriously will remain barren (Deuteronomy 8:11–14). A people that remembers the great and mighty deeds of the Lord will be blessed (Deuteronomy 8:18). A people that forgets is doomed to frustration and failure (Deuteronomy 8:19–20). In fact, the whole direction of a culture depends on the gracious appointments of memory:

> Wonders cannot be known in the midst of darkness.
> Righteousness cannot be done in a land of forgetfulness.
> (Psalm 88:12)

That is why the Bible makes it plain that there are only two kinds of people in the world: *effectual doers* and *forgetful hearers* (James 1:25). And that is why the ministry of the Holy Spirit in the lives of believers is primarily to bring to our *remembrance* the Word of Truth (John 14:26).

Philip Schaff, the prolific church historian during the previous generation, argued stridently that we must be eternally vigilant in the task of handing on our great legacy—

to remember and then to inculcate that remembrance in the hearts and minds of our children:

> How shall we labor with any effect to build up the church, if we have no thorough knowledge of its history, or fail to apprehend it from the proper point of observation? History is, and must ever continue to be, next to God's Word, the richest foundation of wisdom, and the surest guide to all successful practical activity.[5]

Indeed, in this ongoing epic struggle for life—in this tortured clash between historic Christianity and ancient paganism—we dare not neglect our rich legacy. And we dare not keep it to ourselves:

> Listen, oh my people, to my instruction; incline your ears to the words of my mouth. I will open my mouth in a parable; I will utter dark sayings of old, which we have heard and known, and our fathers have told us. We will not conceal them from our children, but tell to the generation to come the praises of the Lord, and His strength and His wondrous works that He has done. For He established a testimony in our midst and appointed a new law in the land, which He commanded to our fathers, that they should teach them to their children that the generation to come might know, even the children yet to be born that they may in turn arise and tell them to their children, that they should put their confidence in God, and not forget the works of God, but keep His commandments. (Psalm 78:1–7)

Seeing that the Spirit has been at work since the time of Christ, we would do well to look back at what He has done. After all, despite our almost adolescent propensity for asserting that the people of all previous centuries could not possibly know how to deal with the dilemmas of modernity, the Church has *successfully* dealt with many of the issues we face today. The fact is that all too often modern Christians are prevented from fully understanding their situation because of their ignorance of their historical context.

Lord Acton, the great Christian historian from the last century, wrote:

> History must be our deliverer not only from the undue influence of other times, but from the undue influence of our own, from the tyranny of the environment and the pressures of the air we breathe.[6]

The English author and lecturer, John H. Y. Briggs, argues that an historical awareness is essential for the health and well-being of any society; it enables us to know who we are, why we are here, and what we should do. He says:

> Just as a loss of memory in an individual is a psychiatric defect calling for medical treatment, so too any community which has no social memory is suffering from an illness.[7]

The Church is a society instituted by Jesus Christ. It is important that members of this society remember the legacy which God has graciously given them.

None of this is to imply that any tradition can speak with the same authority as Scripture does, of course. But it does speak with enough authority that we should pay careful heed. Jordan explains that:

> Not all the prayers, music, and theology of the traditions are equally good. Not everything said in the past is of equal value. It is the Bible that judges the traditions.

Nevertheless, the traditions play an important part in the life of the Christian.

> It is simply not possible for every individual Christian theologian to rethink every doctrinal and ethical matter out of the Bible. We rely on customs and traditions, on historic creeds and confessions, to do a lot of the work for us. Only when we face a serious crisis do we go back to the Bible and question our traditions.[8]

So, what view has the Christian Church traditionally held through the centuries? What did the pioneers of our faith have to say about the issue of homosexuality?

The Ancient and Medieval Church

The early Church's view of homosexuality was unhesitating and unanimous. Referring to the writings of the early Church from the first century forward, the Anglican bishop of Crediton, England, Peter Coleman asserts:

> Although the evidence is sparse, documents surviving from that period usually express undeviating hostility, and show that the leaders of the Church were aware of homosexual practices and firmly opposed to what they considered an immoral aspect of the pagan society in which they lived.[9]

Richard Hays of Yale Divinity School concurs:

> Every pertinent Christian text from the pre-Constantinian period . . . adopts an unremittingly negative judgment on homosexual practice, and this tradition is emphatically carried forward by all the major Christian writers of the fourth and fifth centuries.[10]

Indeed, the Christian apologist Athenagoras wrote to the emperors Marcus Aurelius and Lucius Aurelius Commodus midway through the second century explaining to them that accusations by the pagans that Christians were sexually immoral were not only false but hypocritical.

> The harlot reproves the chaste. Our accusers have set up a market for fornication, have established infamous houses of every sort of shameful pleasure for the young, and do not even spare the males—males committing shocking acts with males. In all sorts of ways they outrage those with the more graceful and handsome bodies. They dishonor God's splendid creation, for beauty on earth is not self-made, but has been created by the hand and mind of God. It is these people who revile us with

the very things they are conscious of in themselves and which they attribute to their gods. They boast of them, indeed, as noble acts and worthy of the gods. Adulterers and corrupters of boys, they insult eunuchs and those once married.[11]

After the conversion of Emperor Constantine, the Christianizing of the Roman Empire and its attendant culture—which had been proceeding apace since the coming of the Holy Spirit on Pentecost—was officially sanctioned. The Christian sexual ethic, therefore, was gradually established as the normative standard for all behavior. Interestingly though, this process was not primarily facilitated by the civil government. Both the behavior and the attitudes of the citizenry were changed by the nurture and the discipline of the local congregations.[12] The Canon law of the early Church established restorative penances for homosexual activity, for instance:

> They who have committed sodomy with men or brutes, murderers, wizards, adulterers, and idolaters, have been thought worthy with these which you do to others. We ought not make any doubt of receiving those who have repented thirty years for the uncleanness which they committed through ignorance; for their ignorance pleads their pardon, and their willingness in confessing it; therefore command them to be forthwith received, especially if they have tears to prevail upon your tenderness, and have since their lapse lived such a life as to deserve your compassion.[13]

While this may seem severe to modern ears, and may attract accusations of "legalism," the Church was, in fact, simply attempting to take sin seriously and to deal with it pastorally. In a society where, for ages, fathers were thought to have a legal right to kill their newborn sons and—more often—daughters if they did not want them, where the state gave slaveholders life-and-death powers over their slaves, where murder in the gladiator pits was a popularly accepted spectator sport, and the political rulers held absolute authority over the lives of their subjects, somehow the Church had to inculcate into the populace a Christian world-and-life view—a Biblical ethic. Theologian Rousas John Rushdoony explains early Christianity's great cultural challenge:

> The early Church had a serious problem, its duty to uphold the law in a lawless age. Men whose offenses required the death penalty . . . remained alive, and their return to the Church posed problems. Where the Biblical law required restitution, the matter was relatively simple, but what of offenses requiring death? Acceptance on a simple declaration of repentance was obviously to make these crimes lighter in their consequences than many lesser offenses. As a result, the penitential system evolved. Protestants, who are accustomed only to see its later flagrant abuses, almost always fail to see its earlier health, and its force as an instrument of law. Acts of penance were required of adulterers, for example, *not* as a work of atonement, but as practical acts of sanctification. The penance served a double purpose. First, it demonstrated the sincerity of the profession of repentance. Second, it constituted a form of restitution. Penance was thus a firm stem towards re-establishing a law-order which the state had denied.[14]

Though the primary responsibility to spread the Christian sexual ethic belonged to the institutional Church, the civil government also had a role to play. Taking the Bible seriously, Christians knew that God punished whole societies with plagues, economic depressions, and wars when they refused to obey or enforce His laws.[15] In 588 A.D. the Emperor Justinian decreed:

> Because of such crime—blasphemy and sodomy—there are famines, earthquakes, and pestilences; wherefore we admonish men to abstain from the aforesaid unlawful acts, that they may not lose their souls . . . We order the most illustrious prefect of the capital to arrest those who

persist in the aforesaid lawless and impious acts after they have been warned by us, and to inflict on them the extreme punishments, so that the city and the State may not come to harm by reason of such wicked deeds.[16]

In 390 A.D., Emperor Theodosius declared sodomy a capital crime and various Christian realms continued to enforce that standard for well over two millennia.[17] There was never a time when a Christian cultural consensus has offered any sort of justification or endorsement for homosexual activity.

The Reformation Tradition

The Protestant Reformation was an attempt to reform the one, true Church and counteract corruptions that had developed within it. Under the slogan *Sola Scriptura,* the reformers attempted to bring the Church in line with the Word of God from which they believed it had departed.

Their call for Reformation touched on every area of life and godliness, including the area of Christian sexual ethics.

Not surprisingly, the Reformers, in maintaining faithfulness to Scripture, never varied from the Biblical standard of heterosexual monogamy. And so, they did not hesitate to condemn homosexuality as sin. For example, Luther, in his commentary on Genesis, asserted:

> The heinous conduct of the people of Sodom is extraordinary, inasmuch as they departed from the natural passion and longing of the male for the female, which was implanted into nature by God, and desired what is altogether contrary to nature. Whence comes this perversity? Undoubtedly from Satan, who, after people have once turned away from the fear of God, so powerfully suppresses nature that he blots out the natural desire that is contrary to nature.[18]

John Calvin, commenting on a passage in Deuteronomy, said:

This passage treats all the infamous sorts of lechery, even the most loathsome kinds of them, whether incest or sodomy, or other such corruptions. And it is with good reason that God chooses out these particular kinds, for it is to the end that we should be touched with the more fear and terror when we go about any kind of lechery.[19]

One of the questions from the *Westminster Larger Catechism* asks: "What are the sins forbidden in the Seventh Commandment?" Sodomy is listed among the correct answers.[20]

Thus, the Reformation Tradition conformed to the traditions of the Ancient and Medieval Church and affirmed with them the Biblical condemnation of homosexuality as sin.

The Modern Church

Sadly, the twentieth century saw this remarkable two-thousand-year-old legacy erode. In an astonishingly short period of time the Church lost control over the culture due to both internal compromise and institutional retreat—capitulating to the juggernaut of inhuman Humanism. According to David Chilton:

Once upon a time, Christians assumed they had a duty to lead the world, to set the standards for society. Christians founded universities, built hospitals, and were at the forefront of scientific activity and social action. Yet the twentieth century has witnessed the Church taking a back seat to the secular Humanists, allowing our enemies to steer us according to their maps and their itineraries, toward their destinations. When today's Church does venture to speak out on social issues, it usually produces little more than a weak echo of the Humanist agenda. Only rarely do we issue manifestoes; our feeble bleatings merely serve as evidence of the new Babylonian Captivity—dressed up with jargon-laden justifications for our bondage to alien worldviews and pagan standards.[21]

The responsibility for the modern situation lies squarely on the Church's doorstep:

> This retreat has been absolutely inexcusable. There is no internal logic in Christianity that requires it to lie down or run out of steam. There is nothing in the nature of the world that makes a flight from victory necessary. There is no eschatological imperative that predetermines the defeat of the Church. On the contrary, our Lord infallibly promised us victory *if we are faithful to Him.*[22]

While there are many ways in which the Church has made itself vulnerable to the onslaught of Humanism, perhaps the most significant has been an idolatrous worship of "science." Even the most conservative Christians in America have yielded to the seductive siren's call of scientism.

Evangelical historian George Marsden, in his compelling essay, "The Collapse of American Evangelical Academia," writes that:

> Among American Protestants there was no crisis of science versus religion associated with the first, or Newtonian, scientific revolution. The American Puritans and their heirs, by and large, embraced the new science with enthusiasm.[23]

The fact is, the nineteenth-century Evangelicals largely based their faith on the evidence of modern science. The problem with much of that science was that it built on the assumptions of Enlightenment ideas which denied the fallen nature of man and asserted that truth could be discovered irrespective of one's theological or ethical commitments. In effect, Evangelicals asserted that Christianity was true *because* it met the standards of modern science.

But like a child playing *Monopoly,* modern science changes the rules as it goes along.[24] Darwin, Freud, Marx and others introduced scientific theories and innovations that were much more blatantly anti-Christian than Newtonianism. As a result, the Christian faith was undercut. Since the Church had already established Christianity on the basis of modern science, it now had to either alter Christianity or give up intellectual prestige.[25]

The Church is still feeling the effect of this compromise of the authority of Scripture with the authority of theoretical science. Recently, for example, a researcher at the Salk Institute for Biological Studies in San Diego, Simon LeVay, discovered a group of cells in the brains of some homosexual men was much smaller than that of some heterosexual men. According to author E. Calvin Beisner:

> The report made headlines nationwide. National Public Radio's report was nothing short of celebratory. ABC's "Nightline" devoted an entire program to it. Why? Because it hints that there is a biological basis for homosexuality. Therefore, it can't be condemned as immoral; it can't be made illegal; it can't be seen as abnormal or sick or disgusting or abominable.[26]

Undoubtedly, LeVay's findings will be cited as authoritative in future denominational debates over sexual ethics, even though the size of his study sample was much smaller than normally required to be considered reliable and even though there is no evidence that the differences cause homosexual behavior and not vice versa. Because LeVay's findings are considered "scientific," all too many in the Church will be all too willing to alter all too much Christian doctrine and ethics accordingly.

Observation is needed in order to increase knowledge, but what is observed must be tested and interpreted through the lens of Scripture. The problem is that even science is filtered through our fallible predispositions, presuppositions, and prejudices. Modern science is built on the claim that experience is the only source of knowledge. As Chilton has written:

> The Bible tells us, on the other hand, that God's Word is the source of knowledge. Our experience can test truth only insofar as our experience is subject to God's Word.[27]

Repentance and Restoration

Thankfully, there are Christians who are resisting the modern trend toward apostasy and bearing witness to what the Gospel teaches about homosexuality.

Regeneration, a Christian group in Baltimore directed by Alan Medinger, has brought about the repentance and restoration of many homosexuals—some of whom are now married with children. Medinger is attempting to start more groups up and down the East Coast but, tragically, his own denomination, the Episcopal Church, is mostly either uncooperative or hostile, while most Evangelicals are sympathetic but unwilling to get actively involved.[28]

White Stone Ministries has an office at Ruggles Baptist Church in Boston where Mike Mitchel and Linda Frank counsel homosexuals who wish to alter their sinful sexual habits. Both know that repentance and restoration is possible because both were once homosexual themselves.[29]

Desert Stream Ministries is located in Santa Monica, California, where it brings a message of repentance and restoration to homosexuals. Its director, Andrew Comiskey, also an ex-homosexual, serves as president of Exodus International, an umbrella organization for over seventy-five similar ministries worldwide which carry the Good News of repentance and restoration to homosexuals.[30]

Ron and Joanne Highley of New York City run L.I.F.E., a Bible-centered ministry to homosexuals. They publish testimonials of the fruits of repentance and restoration, including heterosexual marriage announcements and reports on the birth of subsequent children.[31]

Jesus People USA is a local Christian community in Chicago which ministers to many groups of people that are often overlooked by more traditional congregations, including homosexuals. They do not let modern science prevent them from presenting a message of repentance and restoration to homosexuals. They write:

The environmental/psychological factors that constitute homosexual behavior are indeed various and complex. Liability is very much a part of this matter. We make choices on how we respond to stimuli. Compulsive behavior is not immune to the scrutiny of eternal judgment either.[32]

Conclusion

The proclamation of the Biblical message on homosexuality has been consistent and clear throughout the centuries. Only in the modern age has the visible Church substantially departed from it. Nevertheless, there is still a remnant being used of God to bring repentance and restoration to homosexuals. Perhaps their example will bring repentance and restoration to the Church of Jesus Christ.

In the present struggle to uphold our two thousand year old heritage, it would stand us in good stead to pay heed to this pattern—this legacy—and to reclaim it.

After all, there is no need to reinvent the wheel. As historian David R. Carlin has said:

The best way to develop an attitude of responsibility toward the future is to cultivate a sense of responsibility toward the past. We are born into a world that we didn't make, and it is only fair that we should be grateful to those who did make it. Such gratitude carries with it the imperative that we preserve and at least slightly improve the world that has been given us before passing it on to subsequent generations. We stand in the midst of many generations. If we are indifferent to those who went before us and actually existed, how can we expect to be concerned for the well-being of those who come after us and only potentially exist?[33]

5

HOW SHOULD
WE THEN LIVE?

nunc aut nunquam [1]

"The word that has no definition is the word that has no substitute." [2]

G.K. Chesterton

O ver three hundred years ago, the great Puritan writer, John Bunyan, began his classic masterpiece, *Pilgrim's Progress,* with a desperate and woeful cry for direction:

> As I walked through the wilderness of this world, I lighted on a certain place where was a den, and I laid me down in that place to sleep, and as I slept I dreamed a dream. I dreamed, and behold I saw a man clothed in rags, standing in a certain place, with his face from his own house, a book in his hand, and a great burden on his back. I looked and saw him open the book, and read therein; and as he read he wept and trembled, and not being able to longer contain, he brake out with a lamentable cry, saying: *What shall I do?* [3]

Over three hundred years later, the cry still arises. The burden still exists. Concerned pilgrims still look out over the "wilderness of this world," seeing the calamities of destruction, irresponsibility, depravity, licentiousness, desperation, privation, debauchery, and blasphemy. They witness a tattered, ragged, and bedraggled humanistic culture gone awry: perversity, poverty, ignorance, tyranny, exploitation, abuse, neglect, and violence. And, not surprisingly they cry out, as if with one voice: *What shall I do? And, how do I do it?*

People want to know how they can make a difference. They want to know how they can help change the minds, hearts, and lives of those around them. They want to know how to integrate a Christian worldview and the nitty gritty details of life in this poor fallen world. They want to find out how they can *actually* do something more significant than writing a letter, giving a donation, or casting a vote. They want to stand for the truth, oppose debauchery, protect the innocent, comfort the distressed, and build for the future. They want to utilize their gifts, abilities, and skills.

But all too often, they just don't know how. Or, the task looks too ominous and they don't know where to start.

And so they cry out: *What shall I do?*

The answer is simple to assert; difficult to fulfill—it is merely to uphold our responsibilities in every area: in the Church, at home, and in the community.

Our Responsibility in the Church

The Church is the most important institution on earth. All other institutions will pass away, but the Church will remain through eternity. The Church is the Bride of Christ (Revelation 21:9–10), loved by Him and united with Him as His own body. It possesses the keys of the Kingdom (Matthew 16:18–19), the authority of the sacraments (Matthew 28:19; 1 Corinthians 12:13; Matthew 26:26–27; 1 Corinthians 10:14–16), and the responsibility to forgive and not to forgive sins (John 20:23). It is a nation of priests (1 Peter 2:9), the holy city of New Jerusalem (Hebrews 22–24), and the discipler of the nations (Matthew 28:19). In both bringing individual sinners to repentance and restoration, and reclaiming our culture by calling for national repentance and

restoration, the institutional Church is of primary importance.

To successfully meet the challenge of the Humanist
and homosexual assaults on our culture it is essential that
the Church recover its proper place, perspective, and purpose—including the true preaching of the Word, the correct administration of the sacraments, and the proper practice of Church discipline. These marks of genuine
spirituality are indispensable.

The true preaching of the Word involves the faithful
exposition of Scripture as it applies to all of life—including
the whole realm of sexual ethics. The Bible clearly condemns homosexuals—along with any and all other practicing sinners—to eternal punishment. It is equally clear that
the Bible promises forgiveness, eternal life, and the Holy
Spirit to those who will "repent, and be baptized in the
name of Jesus Christ for the remission of sins" (Acts 2:38).
Both these truths must be expounded without compromise.
If the Church is to be faithful to Christ, it must proclaim
the whole counsel of God—Law and Gospel, Wrath and
Grace, Holiness and Love.

Yet Christians must not reduce the Church's ministry to
a mere message, as important as that message might be.
The Church as an institution is meant for more than a
method of proclamation. It is also a means of incorporation. It is the Church, as the *Westminster Confession* states,
"through which all men are saved and union with which is
essential to their best growth and service."[4]

The sacraments are an important element of the union
of believers with the Church and of the union of the
Church with Christ. Baptism and the Lord's Supper "put a
visible difference between those that belong unto the
Church and the rest of the world."[5] It is through baptism
that we "wash away our sins, calling on the name of the
Lord" (Acts 27:16) and are made part of the Church. It is
through the Lord's Supper "that Christ's flesh, separated
from us by such a great distance, penetrates to us, so that it

becomes our food" and "by which Christ pours His life into us, as if it penetrated into our bones and marrow."[6] As Jesus stated:

> Most assuredly, I say to you, unless you eat the flesh of the Son of Man and drink His blood, you have no life in you. Whoever eats My flesh and drinks My blood has eternal life, and I will raise him up at the last day. For My flesh is food indeed, and My blood is drink, indeed. He who eats My flesh and drinks My blood abides in Me and I in him. As the living Father has sent Me, and I live because of the Father, so he who feeds on Me will live because of Me. This is the bread which came down from heaven—not as your fathers ate the manna and are dead. He who eats this bread will live forever. (John 6:53–58)

Any Christian outreach to homosexuals must make the Church and the sacraments central to their ministry. This is especially important to those who have been heavily involved in habitual sin which has corrupted the core of their own character. People who struggle with their own identity need a new context in which to understand their new position in Christ. Christians can best provide this through incorporation in the institutional Church—by emphasizing the sacraments. Baptism manifests the purifying work of the Spirit in washing away our old selves and the putting on of the new. The Lord's Supper manifests our union with Christ by virtue of His sacrifice on our behalf. Author Rick Ritchie argues:

> We can be saved by merely trusting that the blood of Christ has paid for our sins, but how much more our faith is strengthened when God offers us the chance to partake of the ransom payment! We do not await a future judgment desperately hoping that some past experience of Christ in our hearts will be remembered. God has declared his favor toward us. If our mental experience of Christ is too ethereal for us to hang onto, our

mouths are made of more solid stuff, and we can receive Christ orally.[7]

It is extremely important, however, that the sacramental blessings of Christ's grace not be given promiscuously. Baptism must not be administered to those who unrepentantly practice sin, for baptism in the Bible is never separated from repentance—from turning away from sin. Likewise, those who, after becoming members of the Church, begin living in sin, must be confronted. The Bible says:

> Moreover if your brother sins against you, go and tell him his fault between you and him alone. If he hears you, you have gained your brother. But if he will not hear you, take with you one or two more, that by the mouth of two or three witnesses every word may be established. And if he refuses to hear them, tell it to the Church. But if he refuses even to hear the Church, let him be to you like a heathen and a tax collector. Assuredly, I say to you, whatever you bind on earth will be bound in heaven, and whatever you loose on earth will be loosed in heaven. (Matthew 18:15–18)

Furthermore, the Apostle Paul, writing to the Church of Corinth about a member who was living in sin, exhorted them:

> In the name of our Lord Jesus Christ, when you are gathered together, along with my spirit, with the power of the Lord Jesus Christ, deliver such a one to Satan for the destruction of the flesh, that his spirit may be saved in the day of the Lord Jesus. (1 Corinthians 5:4–5)

Those baptized into the Church who fall into sin and refuse to repent must be disciplined and discipled. They must be disbarred from the Lord's Supper—for their own sake as well as for the Church's (1 Corinthians 11:28–31). This is not optional. As Paul warned the Thessalonian Church, "But we command you, brethren, in the name of our Lord Jesus Christ, that you withdraw from every

brother who walks disorderly and not according to the tradition he received from us" (2 Thessalonians 3:6).

A Church which does not properly discipline and disciple the unrepentant—but instead promiscuously tolerates
them—is in grave danger. Jesus threatened the Church of
Pergamum, "because you have there those who hold to the
doctrine of Balaam, who taught Balak to put a stumbling
block before the children of Israel, to eat things sacrificed
to idols, and to commit sexual immorality," and told them,
"Repent, or else I will come to you quickly and will fight
them with the sword of my mouth" (Revelation 2:14, 16.
See also 2:20–24).

The Church must not only practice discipline, but restoration as well. Of those who have been excommunicated
but then repent, the Apostle Paul wrote:

> This punishment which was inflicted by the majority is suf-
> ficient for such a man, so that, on the contrary, you ought
> rather forgive and comfort him, lest perhaps such a one be
> swallowed up with too much sorrow. Therefore, I urge you
> to reaffirm your love to him. (2 Corinthians 2:6–9)

According to this passage, there are at least three steps
to full restoration.

First, the sinner is to be truly forgiven. That means that
the sin will never be held against him. It must not be re-
peated to him or to others. It must not be stored away as
the basis for a grudge. The case is closed, period.

Secondly, the Church must "comfort him." The Greek
word used here is *parakaleo*, which actually means to help,
assist, counsel, and persuade, as well as comfort. Christian
counselor Jay Adams says that that sort of Biblical "comfort" may involve pastoral care and nurture:

> Counseling about the problems and the sins that led to
> their ouster in the first place. Help in becoming
> reassimilated into the body. Help in making new social
> contacts and reinstating old ones. Help in reconciling

themselves to others to whom they spoke hard words or toward whom they did despicable things. They will need guidance in finding their place in the body so that they can once again begin to use their gifts—none of this business about making them wait six months to rejoin the choir! They may need medical assistance; Satan can be rough, and if they have been in his hands any length of time, they will probably bear the marks that show it. They may need financial help.[8]

Finally, the repentant person must be formally reinstated to fellowship in the Church. He should be given back all rights and privileges of Church membership and, most importantly, be admitted to full communing status. Again, according to Adams:

> This does not mean, of course, that he can simply leap back into the saddle of leadership: office-bearing is not an automatic right of membership. But it must be made clear, to both the congregation and the repentant person, that he is being joyfully received back into full fellowship within the covenant family, once again in complete communion with Christ and His people.[9]

Remember, the Church—though it must truthfully represent Christ's wrath—is primarily an institution of grace. The predominant purpose of Church discipline is repentance and restoration.

Sadly, there are a number of obstacles that inhibit the exercise of Church discipline today. And chief among those obstacles is the very structure of Church organization: denominationalism. Theologian John Frame comments that "those churches that seek to implement Biblical discipline are frequently frustrated by denominationalism."[10] Why? Because it is all too easy and all too common in America today for a person to leave a Church in which he has come under discipline and simply go down the street to another. All too few churches actually ask prospective members for a letter of good standing from their last

Church. Denominational barriers make this already difficult intercongregational communication worse. It may even
"foster an ungodly competitiveness, rather than coopera-
tiveness,"[11] which makes discipline even more ineffectual.

There are, however, some ways of dealing with the
problems brought about by these kinds of divisions.
Churches need to recognize the discipline of other
churches—even those of different denominations whenever possible and wherever legitimate. Otherwise, the importance of the Church's power and authority to discipline
and disciple cannot be realized. In the case of denominations that differ significantly in theology, if a person says he
was forced to leave a church because of his theological confession, the church to which he is applying for membership
should investigate his story before accepting him. The present assault on the integrity of the Gospel and the Church
can only be thwarted by a united Church.

Additionally, the Church has a clear mandate to minister to those who suffer as a consequence of their sin and to
those who are victims of the sins of others. That is why, for
instance, AIDS should be seen as an opportunity for ministry—not a threat to it. Historically, it was the institutional
Church which founded hospitals as a natural outgrowth of
the Gospel. To this day, many hospitals bear religious
names. The Church needs to fully recover its legacy:

> The task of evangelism doesn't end with a proclamation
> of the Gospel. As important as that is, the Bible makes it
> plain that if we want to win the world for Christ we are
> going to have to match our words with deeds. We are
> going to have to authenticate the claims of the Gospel
> with *holy activity*. Faith without corresponding works is al-
> together worthless. It is in fact dead.[12]

Our Responsibility at Home

The family is a divine institution, which—though not, like
the Church, eternal—is immensely important to the tempo-

ral welfare of a culture and the fulfillment of the Cultural Mandate. That mandate was addressed to the family:

> Be fruitful and multiply; fill the earth and subdue it; have dominion over the fish of the sea, over the birds of the air, and over every living thing that moves across the earth. (Genesis 1:26–28, 2:24)

The Biblical family consists of a faithful relationship between one man and one woman. Obviously, this definition is under attack today, as author Gary DeMar notes:

> There are, what Alvin Toffler calls, a bewildering array of family forms: homosexual marriages, communes, groups of elderly people banding together to share expenses and sometimes sex, tribal groupings among certain ethnic minorities, and many other forms coexist as never before. These counterfeit families attempt to restructure the family around an evolving order rather than a Biblical model.[13]

The most important resource the Christian family has that the homosexual movement can never counter or subvert is *children:*

> Behold, children are a heritage from the LORD, the fruit of the womb is his reward. Like arrows in the hand of a warrior, so are the children of one's youth. Happy is the man who has his quiver full of them; they shall not be ashamed, but shall speak with their enemies in the gate. (Psalm 127:3–5)

It is essential, therefore, for families to take whatever means necessary to protect their best witnesses for the Biblical sexual ethic—their own progeny.

The opponents of the Christian sexual ethic are well aware of the importance of the Biblical family. That is why it is so important to the homosexual lobby to get their agenda put into the classrooms under the guise of either health or sex education. Congressman William Dannemeyer says:

Clearly they see the "explicit" and "nonjudgmental" sex education as a means of introducing young people to the practices of homosexuals. To "avoid bigotry" the public schools are being enjoined to teach heterosexuality and homosexuality without bias. In fact, since, according to homosexuals, they are victims of widespread "homophobia" as the result of "outmoded religious prejudices," they are demanding that their behavior be defended and their rights affirmed *in American classrooms*. In a curriculum that is supposed to be "value free," they want tolerance of homosexual behavior elevated to the level of a moral imperative.[14]

Using the public schools to socialize children with a non-Christian worldview is nothing new. Recently, however, the perversity of public education has increased so much that more and more Christian parents are hard pressed to overlook it any longer and are searching for viable alternatives.

According to Scripture, the education of children is the responsibility of the parents. Children are exhorted not to keep company with sinners but to listen instead to their parents. Parents ought not, therefore, give their children over to ethical subverters for over six hours a day. Jesus stressed the immensity of our responsibility to children when He said that:

> Whoever causes one of these little ones who believe in Me to sin, it would be better for him if a millstone were hung around his neck, and he were drowned in the depth of the sea. (Matthew 18:6)

Ensuring a consistently Christian education for their children is a vital task that all Christian families need to carry out. This education must include not only reading, writing, and arithmetic, but also the modeling of Biblical gender roles.[15]

Our Responsibility in the Community

There was a long period in the early to mid-twentieth century when Evangelicals eschewed involvement in politics. More recently, however, Christians are beginning to awaken to their responsibility to "make disciples of all the nations" (Matthew 28:19). Had Christians never lost their vision of a Christian society, perhaps we would not be in the mess we currently find ourselves in.

Sadly, this new surge in Christian political activism has been forced into a primarily negative posture—that is, it has been forced into a defensive mode. We have had to oppose attempts by federal, state, and local governments to force us to accept homosexuality as a legitimate lifestyle. We have had to oppose housing codes that penalize Christian landlords who refuse to rent facilities to people who have adopted sinful practice as their way of life. We have had to oppose the use of tax monies to fund homosexual pornographic propaganda. We have had to oppose attempts by the government to punish those who attempt, in their home or workplace, to avoid contracting AIDS from those infected with it. We have had to oppose "hate crime" legislation which attempts to penalize people for their opinions of homosexuality. We have had to oppose school curriculums that portray the homosexual lifestyle as a legitimate option. In essence, we have had to oppose the use of government coercion by the homosexual lobby to force us to conform to their agenda.

As necessary as this defensive posture has been, it cannot be anything but a short-term strategy. As Christians, our long-term goals for the civil government must include the positive enforcement of justice as defined by Scripture. Jesus Christ is not just the Head of the Church, but He is also the King of kings and Lord of lords (Revelation 19:16).

> Now therefore, be wise, O kings; be instructed, you judges of the earth. Serve the LORD with fear, and re-

joice with trembling. Kiss the Son, lest He be angry, and
you perish in the way, when His wrath is kindled but a
little. Blessed are all those who put their trust in Him.
(Psalm 2:10–12)

As the awful scourge of AIDS amply demonstrates,
when a culture departs from Christ's standard of justice,
frightful consequences are meted out to the wicked and
the innocent alike. It is essential to the health and welfare
of our civilization that we be governed by God's Word, not
man's word. We must therefore attempt to elect represen-
tatives who take the Bible seriously and we must put forward a positive program of civil justice and corporate
mercy. To begin with, this means campaigning for the restoration of moral constraint laws—ranging from alimony
exaction precepts to anti-sodomy statutes.[16]

Right and Wrong

It is the sad tendency of modern men to either do the
right thing in the wrong way or to do the wrong thing in
the right way. We either hold to the truth obnoxiously or
we hold to a lie graciously. We are either a rude angel or a
polite devil. Often what poses as a cruel orthodoxy is defeated by what poses as a kind heresy.

That is what makes the current debate over sexual ethics so terribly complex. Those that hold to the Biblical standard are often anything but the picture of Christian deco-
rum. While those that play fast and free with the moral
tenor of the faith are often generous to a fault.

Thus, it is not enough to simply assert that Christians
do what God wants them to do—in the Church, in the
state, and in the home. They must be what God wants
them to be as well.

According to the *Westminster Confession of Faith,* the
Church has been entrusted with, "the ministry, oracles, and
ordinances of God, for the gathering and perfecting of the

saints, in this life, to the end of the world."[17] In order to faithfully carry out this stewardship wisely, the mission of the Church must be organized around what Francis Schaeffer called "two contents, two realities."[18]

The first content is sound doctrine. The Church must teach it, exhort it, nurture it, and highlight it in all that it does in both its evangelism and its discipleship, from its worship to its societal presence.

The second content is honest answers to honest questions. The Great Commission and the Cultural Mandate are the Church's highest priorities in its mission to the world. They must be carried out, perpetrated, and perpetuated in gentleness, openness, kindness, and helpfulness.

The first reality is true spirituality. Holiness, godliness, and spiritual discipline must be the distinctive marks of the true Church. Thus, prayer, fasting, almsgiving, and fixedness in the Word should be just as evident in the lives of the members as fervent evangelism and glorious worship.

The second reality is the beauty of human relationships. Within the Church there should be abundant evidence of true *koinonia*. At the same time, relations between the Church and the community should show forth service, tenderness, understanding, empathy, and compassion.

Thus while an unswerving commitment to truth must be maintained in the Church—it must be contextualized by an equally unswerving commitment to servanthood.

Without that, right appears to be wrong while wrong appears to be right.

The Story of the Good Samaritan

It was supposed to be a test. Straightforward. Simple. A test of orthodoxy. A test of theological skillfulness. Not a trap, really. Just a test:

> And behold, a certain lawyer stood up and put Jesus to the test, saying, "Teacher, what shall I do to inherit eter-

nal life?" And He answered him, "What is written in the law? How does it read to you?" And he answered and said, "You shall love the Lord your God with all your heart, and with all your soul, and with all your strength, and with all your mind; and your neighbor as yourself." And He said to him, "You have answered correctly; do this, and you will live." (Luke 10:25–28)

Christ's word-perfect-never-miss-a-beat response should have been music to the ears of any good Pharisee. He unhesitatingly upheld the Mosaic Law. He was careful "not to exceed what is written" (1 Corinthians 4:6). He was impeccably orthodox.

If that were the end of the story, it would be less a story than a dry recitation of doctrine: true, good, and necessary, but not particularly gripping. But of course, the story doesn't end there.

The lawyer just wouldn't let Jesus off the hook. He continued to cross-examine the Lord. He pressed the issue. Sinful men love to do this. They want God on the hot seat. They want God in the dock.

But he was determined that Jesus wouldn't make him look like a fool:

> Wishing to justify himself, he said to Jesus, "And who is my neighbor?" Jesus replied and said, "A certain man was going down from Jerusalem to Jericho, and he fell among robbers, and they stripped him and beat him, and went off leaving him half dead. And by chance a certain priest was going down on that road, and when he saw him, he passed by on the other side. And likewise a Levite also, when he came to the place and saw him, passed by on the other side. But a certain Samaritan, who was on a journey, came upon him; and when he saw him, he felt compassion, and came to him, and bandaged up his wounds, pouring oil and wine on them, and he put him on his own beast, and brought him to an inn, and took care of him. And on the next day he took out two denarii and gave them to the innkeeper

and said, 'Take care of him; and whatever more you spend, when I return, I will repay you.' Which of these three do you think proved to be a neighbor to the man who fell into the robbers' hands?" And he said, "The one who showed mercy toward him." And Jesus said to him, "Go and do the same." (Luke 10:29–37)

What started out to be a test—a theological confrontation over the law—was suddenly transformed by the Lord Jesus into a moment of conviction. The Pharisee found himself in the valley of decision. And at the same time he was on the horns of a dilemma—because of a Samaritan of all things.

Seven hundred years earlier, Assyria had overrun and depopulated the northern kingdom of Israel, including Samaria. The conquerors had a cruel policy of population-transfer that scattered the inhabitants of the land to the four winds. Then, the empty countryside was repopulated with a ragtag collection of vagabonds and scalawags from the dregs of the Empire (2 Kings 17:24–41). Instead of regarding these newcomers as prospects for Jewish evangelism, the people of Judah, who continued in independence for another full century, turned away in contempt, and the racial division between Samaritan and Jew began its bitter course.

The Samaritans were universally despised by good Jews. They were half-breeds who observed a half-breed religious cultus. Worse than the pagan Greeks, worse even than the barbarian Romans, the Samaritans were singled out by the Jews as a perfect example of despicable depravity. They were close enough geographically and culturally to know of the truth, yet they resisted. Therefore they had no excuse. At least in the eyes of the Jews.

But now, Jesus was elevating a Samaritan to a position of great respect and honor. A Samaritan was the good neighbor, the hero of the parable. According to their way of reckoning, Jesus was thus slapping the religious leaders of Israel in their collective faces.

After demanding an expansion of Christ's textbook answer, the Pharisee might have expected a parable that encouraged him to show love to all men, even to Samaritans. But never in a thousand years would he have guessed that Christ would show how such a despised one could be nearer to the Kingdom than a pious, but compassionless Jew.

The Pharisee asked a passive question, expecting a passive answer: "Who is my neighbor?" (Luke 10:29). But Jesus responded with an active command: "Go and do the same." (Luke 10:37). In other words, Jesus did not supply the teacher with information about whom he should or shouldn't help, because failure to keep the Commandment springs not from a lack of information, but a lack of obedience and love. It was not keener understanding that the teacher needed, but a new heart. Like that of the Samaritan.

Both Law and Love

The Samaritan in the story is a paragon of virtue. He strictly observed the Law, shaming the priest and Levite who "passed by on the other side" (Luke 10:31–32). He paid attention to the needs of others (Deuteronomy 22:4) and showed concern for the poor (Psalm 41:1). He showed pity toward the weak (Psalm 72:13) and rescued them from violence (Psalm 72:14). Knowing the case of the helpless (Proverbs 29:7), he gave of his wealth (Deuteronomy 26:12–13), and shared his food (Proverbs 22:9).

But perhaps even more significant than his strict adherence to the Law, was the compassion that the Samaritan demonstrated.

He wasn't simply "going by the rules." His was not a dry, passionless obedience. He had "put on a heart of compassion, kindness, humility, gentleness, and patience" (Colossians 3:12). He "became a father to the needy, and took up the case of the stranger" (Job 29:16). He loved his neighbor as himself (Mark 12:31), thus fulfilling the Law (Romans 13:10).

The Samaritan fulfilled the demands of both Law *and* love. He demonstrated both obedience and mercy. He heeded the Spirit *and* the letter. He combined faithfulness *and* compassion. He had wed Word and deed.

At another time, Jesus was asked to summarize the Law of God—the standard against which all spirituality is to be measured. He replied:

> You shall love the Lord your God with all your heart, and soul, and mind. This is the great and foremost commandment. And the second is like it; you shall love your neighbor as yourself. On these two commandments depend the law and the prophets. (Matthew 22: 37–40)

Jesus reduced the whole of the Law—and thus, the whole of the faith—to love. Love toward God, and then, love toward man. But at the same time, Jesus defined love in terms of law.

In one bold deft stroke, He freed the Christian faith from both legalism and subjectivism. By linking Law and love, Christ unclouded our purblind vision of both. Love was held in check by responsible objectivity while law was held in check by passionate applicability.

That is the faith of the Good Samaritan—faithful but compassionate, unswerving but merciful, obedient but kind—because that is "the faith once and for all delivered to the saints" (Jude 3).

If we desire to manifest genuine faith before a watching world, this kind of fidelity must be our hallmark. If we ever hope to bear witness to the unadulterated Gospel, we must "speak the truth." But we must do it "in love" (Ephesians 4:15).

That is the only way that right can truly be right and wrong can truly be wrong.

Conclusion

Clearly, the Church is the most important institution in any society. Thus, an agenda for Christian action must begin with the reformation and restoration of the institutional Church. To focus our attention primarily on other things—as fine as they may be—is an unbiblical strategy. As David Chilton has said:

> We know the story of Israel. God forced Pharaoh to release them, and they went on to inherit the Promised Land. But the really crucial aspect of the whole Exodus event, as far as the people's activity was concerned, was *worship*. The orthodox Christian faith cannot be reduced to personal experiences, academic discussions, or culture-building activity—as important as all these are in varying degrees. The essence of Biblical religion is the worship of God. And by worship I do not only mean listening to sermons, even though preaching is certainly necessary and important. I mean *organized, congregational prayers, praise, and sacramental celebration.* This means, further, that the reformation of *Church government* is crucial to Biblical dominion. True Christian reconstruction of culture is far from being simply a matter of passing Law X and electing Congressman Y. Christianity is not a political cult. It is the divinely ordained worship of the Most High God.[19]

In regard to the homosexual agenda: "If our *central* response is social or political action, we are, *in principle,* atheists; we are confessing our faith in human action as the ultimate determiner of history."[20] Even so, it is important we make an uncompromising stand for truth in both the family and the civil government as well. These institutions belong under Christ's Lordship as much as the Church does. "For the earth is the LORD's and everything in it" (Psalm 24:1).

But, if we merely assert the truth, we have only done half our job. God has not called us to be mere citadels of fidelity. He has not called us to be mere bastions of veracity. We are to be winsome ambassadors as well. Thus, when we answer Bunyan's age-old cry, both Word and deed must therefore be evident—both faithfulness and compassion.

That—and that alone—is the authentic Christian faith. That—and that alone—is sufficient for the day.

CONCLUSION: LANCE'S REPRISE

fide et fiducia [1]

"And after our greatest dangers there remaineth a rest." [2]

G.K. Chesterton

T here is no peace for the wicked" (Isaiah 48:22, 57:21). With that booming phrase, the great evangelical prophet Isaiah punctuated his final series of sermons to his beloved people, the citizens of Judah. With a remarkable economy of words, Isaiah was able to capture the essence of his concerns. He was able to summarize his life's message. He was able to outline his theology. He was able to illustrate with absolute clarity the spiritual emphasis of his entire ministry.

All that, in one phrase.

Isaiah—as a true prophet—had dedicated himself to proclaiming to the people God's eternal purposes for them. He was a diligent bearer of the glad tidings of peace. God had established a "covenant of peace" with the people (Isaiah 54:10). And it was an irrevocable, everlasting covenant (Isaiah 61:8). Thus, they would be at peace with the nations (Isaiah 26:12) and at peace with God (Isaiah 27:5). They would have "peace like a river" (Isaiah 66:12) and peace "like the waves of the sea" (Isaiah 48:18). There would be "peace to him who is far off and peace to him who is near" (Isaiah 57:19). It would be a "perfect peace" (Isaiah 26:3) wrought by the "Prince of Peace" (Isaiah 9:6).

But, Isaiah was quick to add, this great and glorious peace would only come upon God's faithful covenant people. "There is no peace for the wicked" (Isaiah 48:22). And sadly, as Isaiah uttered this phrase, the citizens of Judah appeared to be anything but God's faithful covenant people. They were treading the darksome path of wickedness.

Their worship had deteriorated into meaningless ritual (Isaiah 1:11–15). They had become proud and complacent (Isaiah 32:10). They tolerated perversion and wickedness in their midst (Isaiah 30:1–3). Even their own hearts were inclined "toward wickedness, to practice ungodliness and to speak error against the Lord, to keep the hungry person unsatisfied and to withhold drink from the thirsty" (Isaiah 32:6). They were flirting with disaster (Isaiah 5:13–17). For, "there is no peace for the wicked" (Isaiah 48:22).

Thus the God of peace commanded the prophet of peace to reiterate, once and for all, the program for peace, saying:

> Cry loudly, do not hold back; raise your voice like a trumpet, and declare to My people their transgression, and to the house of Jacob their sins. Is this not the fast I choose? To loosen the bonds of wickedness? To undo the bands of the yoke, to let the oppressed go free, and break every yoke? Is it not to divide your bread with the hungry, and bring the homeless poor into the house? When you see the naked, to cover him, and not to hide yourself from your own flesh? Then your light will break out like the dawn, and your recovery will speedily spring forth. And your righteousness will go before you. The glory of the Lord will be your rear guard. Then you will call, and the Lord will answer. You will cry, and He will say, "Here I am." If you remove the yoke from your midst, the pointing of the finger, and speaking wickedness, and if you give yourself to the hungry, and satisfy

the desire of the afflicted, then your light will rise in darkness, and your gloom will become like midday. And the Lord will continually guide you, and satisfy your desire in scorched places, and give strength to your bones. And you will be like a watered garden, like a spring of water whose waters do not fail. And those from among you will build the ancient ruins. You will raise up the age-old foundations. And you will be called the repairer of the breach, and the restorer of the streets in which to dwell. (Isaiah 58:1, 6–12)

Did the people want peace, perfect peace, the peace that surpasses all understanding? Did they want to reconstruct their culture, restore the foundations, and reclaim their lost legacy? Then they would have to repent of their wickedness and do the works of righteousness. They would have to show forth the fruits of grace. They would have to uphold their covenant responsibility. They would have to do what God had called them to do. And they would have to be what God had called them to be.

Lance understood that only too well.

But of course, that had not always been the case. For the longest time, he resisted God's pattern for peace with all his might—for both his own life and for the lives of others. But even then, he did not have a theory so much as a thirst. And ultimately that thirst drove him to the Fountain of Peace in spite of his precious obstinate dogma—a dogma that actually denied that the fountain even existed.

It was only as he began to drink that he realized that such a dogma was in fact a creed of pure caprice. And it was only as he began to drink that he realized how dangerous are those who propose such dogmas in opposition to the true pattern of peace.

"I just came to the place where I realized that being nice and tolerant and accepting were perhaps the cruelest things I could ever be," he told me. "I came to the place where I realized that I was doing my old homosexual friends no favors at all by standing idly by while they not only crippled their own lives but wreaked havoc on the Church and on the culture at large. I came to the place where I realized that the most compassionate thing I could do was to stand firm on the everlasting truth of Almighty God. I must take my place among His faithful covenant people. I don't really have any other choice. After all, there is no peace for the wicked—and wickedness in times like these has to be defined as standing in the wings, doing nothing while all the world struggles under the weight of falsehood and injustice."

From Here to There

At a time when disintegrating forces of deception and perversity are raging all across the cultural landscape, the urgency of peacemaking—of coming to the place of faithfulness and compassion—becomes all too evident. But, no matter what we do, no matter how hard we try, and no matter what we say, a turn-around won't happen overnight. Peace isn't won in a day.

Even at Jericho, when God miraculously delivered the city into the hands of His people, they had to march around the walls for days on end. They had to wait.

Cultural restoration is a multigenerational task. It takes time. It takes work.

Jonathan knew that. So he did not hesitate—not even for a moment. He went to work immediately. He understood the urgency of the situation, so he acted boldly. He knew that the restraints of time demanded decisiveness.

Israel was laboring under the terrible bondage of the Philistines. The army of Jonathan's father, Saul, was defenseless and demoralized, owning no swords, and no spears:

> So it came about on the day of battle that neither sword nor spear was found in the hands of any of the people

who were with Saul and Jonathan, but they were found
with Saul and his son Jonathan. (1 Samuel 13:22)

Imagine that. An entire army with no weapons. Only
the king and his son had any really efficient armaments.
No power. No resources. No army. No decent weapons. No
hope?

Perhaps the people should wait for another day to work
for their deliverance. Perhaps they should wait for the day
of advantage. Perhaps they should do nothing for now, waiting for a more opportune moment. After all, cultural restoration *doesn't* happen overnight. Peace *isn't* won in a day.

But, no. Not Jonathan.

Perhaps God desires for his people to "walk by faith
and not by sight" (2 Corinthians 5:7). "Perhaps," thought
Jonathan, "the Lord will work for us, for the Lord is not
restrained to save by many or by few" (1 Samuel 14:6).

So he set out, just he and his armor bearer, alone, to
attack the Philistine garrison. To gain the promised "peace
of the land." The story is exciting just in the retelling:

> Then Jonathan said, "Behold, we will cross over to the
> men and reveal ourselves to them. If they say to us, 'Wait
> until we come to you,' then we will stand in our place
> and not go up to them. But if they say, 'Come, up to us,'
> then we will go up, for the Lord has given them into our
> hands; and this shall be the sign to us." And when both
> of them revealed themselves to the garrison of the Philis-
> tines, the Philistines said, "Behold, Hebrews are coming
> out of the holes where they have hidden themselves." So
> the men of the garrison hailed Jonathan and his armor
> bearer and said, "Come up to us and we will tell you
> something." And Jonathan said to his armor bearer,
> "Come up after me, for the Lord has given them into
> the hands of Israel." Then Jonathan climbed up on his
> hands and feet, with his armor bearer behind him; and
> they fell before Jonathan, and his armor bearer put
> some to death after him. And that first slaughter which
> Jonathan and his armor bearer made was about twenty

men within about half a furrow in an acre of land. And there was a trembling in the camp, in the field, and among all the people. Even the garrison and the raiders trembled, and the earth quaked so that it became a great trembling. (1 Samuel 14:8–15)

The odds were against him. One man with his armor bearer, against the entire Philistine garrison. It was suicidal.

Maybe. It looked that way. But then, looks can be deceiving. Appearances *are* sometimes quite out of line with facts.

So, what were the facts?

Jonathan knew that the land belonged to God, not to the Philistines (Psalm 24:1). He knew that God had placed the land into the care of His chosen people, the Jews (Joshua 1:2). He knew that they had sure and secure promises that if they would obey God's Word and do God's work, they would be prosperous and successful (Joshua 1:8), that every place which the sole of their feet trod would be granted to them (Joshua 1:3), and that no man would be able to stand before them all the days of their lives (Joshua 1:5). He knew that if the people would only "dwell in the shelter of the Most High," in the "shadow of the Almighty" (Psalm 91:1), He would deliver them "from the snare of the trapper and from the deadly pestilence" (Psalm 91:3). He would cover them "with his pinions" (Psalm 91:4), and protect them from "the terror by night" and "the arrow that flies by day" (Psalm 91:5). And though a thousand fall at their left hand, ten thousand to the right, affliction would not approach them; they would only look and see "the recompense of the wicked" (Psalm 91:7–8). They would be protected from the teeth of the devourer, encompassed with supernatural power (Psalm 91:10).

These were the facts.

Though it looked as if God's people were broken, scattered, defeated, and woe begotten, in truth they were more than conquerors (Romans 9:37). They were overcomers (1 John 5:4). Philistine dominion was fiction. Israel cowering in fear was foolish fantasy. Pessimism about their ability to stand and not be shaken was novel nonsense (Hebrews 12:28). Jonathan knew that. So, he acted. He acted boldly. He acted decisively. He acted on the basis of the truth and reliability of God's Word, not on the seemingly impossible circumstances that faced him. He acted on faith and not on sight. He acted realistically, knowing that God's definition of things is the real reality, the only reality. He acted with passion and zeal for the things he knew to be God's will.

And God honored him. He blessed Jonathan with great success. Unbelievable success.

Jonathan stood against the tide. By all rights, he should have been crushed under its weight, but instead, the tide turned. He won the day and saved the nation.

Faith and Victory

"Now faith is the assurance of things hoped for, the conviction of things not seen" (Hebrews 11:1). "By it the men of old gained approval" (Hebrews 11:2). Against all odds, against all hope they obtained victory. They snatched glory out of the jaws of despair. They hurdled insurmountable obstacles to "lay hold" of the good things of the Lord (Hebrews 6:18). By faith, they believed God for the remarkable, for the impossible (Matthew 19:26; Hebrews 11:1–40): Abraham (Genesis 12:1–4), Sarah (Genesis 18:11–14), Isaac (Genesis 27:27–29), Jacob (Genesis 48:1–20), Joseph (Genesis 50:24–26), Moses (Exodus 14:22–29), Rahab (Joshua 6:23), Ruth (Ruth 1:16–17), Gideon (Judges 6–8), Barak (Judges 4–5), Samson (Judges 13–16), Jephthah (Judges 11–12), David (1 Samuel 16–17), Isaiah (Isaiah 1–6), Samuel, and all the prophets (1 Samuel 1; Hebrews 11:32). For by faith they "conquered kingdoms, performed acts of righteousness, obtained promises, shut the mouths of lions, quenched the power of fire, escaped the edge of the sword, from weakness were made strong, became mighty in war, and put foreign armies to flight" (Hebrews 12:33–34). Though they were mocked and persecuted, imprisoned and tortured, impoverished and oppressed, they were unshaken and eventually obtained God's great reward (Hebrews 11:35–40).

> Therefore, since we have so great a cloud of witnesses surrounding us, let us also lay aside every encumbrance, and the sin which so easily entangles us, and let us run with endurance the race that is set before us, fixing our eyes on Jesus, the author and perfecter of faith, who for the joy set before Him endured the cross, despising the shame, and has sat down at the right hand of the throne of God. (Hebrews 12:1–2)

The future is ours.

But the days are urgent. Humanism's empire of perversity and idolatry, of greed and gluttony, is collapsing like a house of cards. Peace is nowhere to be found.

The battlefields of Europe, Southeast Asia, Central America, and the Middle East give vivid testimony that Humanism's hope for peace on earth is a false hope. The economic ruin of Nicaragua, Ethiopia, Afghanistan, Poland, and Russia give vivid testimony that Humanism's hope for utopia is a false hope. The ovens of Auschwitz, the aborturaries of L.A., the bathhouses of New York, and the nurseries of Bloomington give vivid testimony that Humanism's hope of medical and genetic perfectibility is a false hope. The ghettos of Detroit, the barrios of West San Antonio, the tent cities of Phoenix, and the slums of St. Louis give vivid testimony that Humanism's hope of winning the "war on poverty" is a false hope.

But the Biblical hope has never yet been found wanting.

So, what are we waiting for?

It must be admitted that "there are giants in the land" (Numbers 13:32) and that "we appear to be grasshoppers in our own sight, and in theirs . . ." (Numbers 13:33).

But, God has given us His promises and established His priorities, laid out His strategies, and illumined His principles. And His program cannot fail.

Time to Go to Work

Jonathan faced the Philistines. He took God at His word. He went to work, and emerged victorious.

Similarly, against all odds, Ehud faced the power of Moab (Judges 3:12–30); Shamgar faced the power of the Philistines (Judges 3:31); Deborah faced the power of Canaan (Judges 4–5); Gideon faced the power of Midian (Judges 6–8); the Apostles faced the power of the Roman empire (Acts 8–28); and each one emerged victorious.

Against all odds.

Isn't is about time for us to demonstrate to an unbelieving world that God can *still* beat the odds? Isn't it about time for us to prove to a fallen and depraved generation that God can raise up a weak and unesteemed people against all odds, and win? Isn't it about time we laid the foundation of peace? Isn't it?

> For though we walk in the flesh, we do not war according to the flesh, for the weapons of our warfare are not of the flesh, but divinely powerful for the destruction of fortresses. We are destroying speculations and every lofty thing raised up against the knowledge of God, and we are taking every thought captive to the obedience of Christ. (2 Corinthians 10:3–5)

In Christ, we are actually overwhelmingly powerful (Ephesians 6:10–18; Romans 8:37–39). Even the gates of hell cannot prevail against us (Matthew 16:8). If, that is, we would only do our job—standing faithfully with the covenant people of God through the ages. If we would only

take the Gospel hope beyond, to "the uttermost parts of
the earth" (Acts 1:8), if we would only "make disciples of
all nations" (Matthew 28:19), if we would only "rebuild the
ancient ruins, raise up the age-old foundations, and repair
the breach" (Isaiah 58:12).

It is time to go to work. It is time to lay the foundations
of peace. We may have to work with few, or even no resources—like Jonathan (1 Samuel 14:6). We may have to
improvise, utilizing less than perfect conditions and less
than qualified workers and less than adequate facilities—
like Nehemiah (Nehemiah 1:20). We may have to battle
the powers that be, the rulers and the principalities—like
Peter, James, and John (Acts 4:20). We may have to go with
what we've got, with no support, no notoriety, and no co-
operation—like Jeremiah (Jeremiah 1:4–10). We may have
to start "in weakness and in fear and in much trembling"
(1 Corinthians 2:3), without "persuasive words of wisdom"
(1 Corinthians 2:4)—like the Apostle Paul (1 Corinthians
2:1). Instead of allowing their limitations and liabilities to
discourage and debilitate them, the heroes of the faith
went to work—God's power being made manifest in their
weakness (1 Corinthians 1:26—29).

It is time for *us* to go to work.

Cultural restoration doesn't happen overnight. Peace
isn't won in a day. So the sooner we get started, the better
off we'll be. The sooner we get started, the quicker the victory will come. In order to get from here to there, we need
to set out upon the road. At the very least.

There will never be an ideal time to *begin* the work that
God has set before us in maintaining the integrity of the
Church—on the issue of sexual morality or a thousand
other fronts. Money is *always* short. Volunteers are *always* at
a premium. Facilities are always either too small, or too in-
flexible, or in the wrong location, or too expensive. There
is *never* enough time, *never* enough energy, and *never*
enough resources.

So what?

Our commission is not dependent upon conditions and restrictions. Our commission is dependent only upon the unconditional promises of God's Word. God has called us to peace (1 Corinthians 7:15), to be peacemakers (Matthew 5:9), "so then let us pursue the things that make for peace" (Romans 14:9).

We should just go. Do what we ought to. We should make peace. Starting *now.*

"There is no peace for the wicked." But if we will do our job, and do it now, then peace shall be reckoned unto us.

Jonathan knew the odds were against him, lopsidedly so, when he faced the Philistines single-handedly. But he also knew that God blessed obedience. He knew that God blessed valor. He knew that God's work done in God's way would never lack for God's provision and protection. So, he set out. And he won. He gained peace for the Land.

"Really, that is what I am depending on," Lance told me recently. "Like Jonathan, I know that I've got an uphill battle—in the Church as well as in the world. But I also know that I've got to walk by faith and not by sight. I've got to walk in the supernatural anointing of Almighty God, casting down strongholds, taking every thought, every word, every deed, every man, woman and child captive for Christ. Again, I really don't have any other choice."

Lance is already an amazing emblem of God's grace. May he be an emblem of God's call upon the Church as well. Amen and Amen.

NOTES

Introduction: Lance's Story

1. "Horror in remembrance."
2. G.K. Chesterton, *Charles Dickens* (London: Sheed and Ward, 1934), p. 24.
3. "To God alone be the glory. Jesus saves."

Chapter 1: The Crack in the Cathedral

1. "Evidence of a Crime."
2. G.K. Chesterton, *Charles Dickens* (London: Sheed and Ward, 1934), p. 42.
3. Michael Scott Horton, *Made in America: The Shaping of Modern American Evangelicalism* (Grand Rapids, MI: Baker Books, 1991).
4. *World*, January 5, 1991.
5. Charles Colson, *The God of Stones and Spiders: Letters to a Church in Exile* (Wheaton, IL: Crossway, 1991).
6. *Houston Post*, August 16, 1991.
7. Ibid.
8. Francis Schaeffer, *The Great Evangelical Disaster* (Wheaton, IL: Crossway Books, 1984).
9. James W. Skillen, *The Scattered Voice: Christians at Odds in the Public Square* (Grand Rapids, MI: Zondervan, 1991).
10. *The New York Times*, August 28, 1991.
11. *National and International Religion Report*, August 12, 1991.
12. *World*, February 23, 1991.
13. *World*, July 27, 1991.
14. *Christianity Today*, August 19, 1991.
15. *National and International Religion Report*, July 22, 1991.
16. Ibid.

17. Ibid.
18. Ibid.
19. *World,* August 10, 1991.
20. *World,* June 29, 1991.
21. Ibid.
22. Ibid.
23. *Christianity Today,* July 22, 1991.
24. Ibid.
25. *World,* February 23, 1991.
26. Ibid.
27. *National and International Religion Report,* August 12, 1991.
28. *National and International Religion Report,* July 29, 1991.
29. *World,* July 13, 1991.
30. John Shelby Spong, *Rescuing the Bible from Fundamentalism: A Bishop Rethinks the Meaning of Scripture* (San Francisco: Harper, 1991).
31. John Shelby Spong, *Living In Sin: A Bishop Rethinks Human Sexuality* (San Francisco: Harper and Row, 1988).
32. *World,* September 29, 1990.
33. *World,* August 10, 1991.
34. David A. Fraser, ed. *The Evangelical Round Table: The Sanctity of Life* (Princeton, NJ: Princeton University Press, 1988). p. 159.
35. Ibid. pp. 160–161. See also: Tony Campolo, *20 Hot Potatoes Christians are Afraid to Touch* (Irving, TX: Word, 1988), pp. 105–120; *Cornerstone,* 19, Issue 94.

Chapter 2: The Storm at Sea

1. "Since the beginning of time."
2. G.K. Chesterton, *Charles Dickens* (London: Sheed and Ward, 1934), p. 36.
3. *Washington Newsletter,* March 1990.
4. *The Rothbard-Rockwell Report,* August 1991.
5. Peter Leithart, *The Promiscuous Society* (unpublished manuscript), pp. 14–15.
6. Ibid.
7. Ibid.
8. *Broward Jewish World,* October 16, 1990.

9. Leithart, p. 73.
10. Carl Becker, *The Heavenly City of Eighteenth-Century Philosophers* (New Haven: Yale University Press, 1932), p. 21.
11. Leithart, p. 65.
12. Jean-Jacques Rousseau, *A Discourse on the Origin of Inequality, in Great Books of the Western World,* Robert Mayneard Hutchins, ed. (Chicago: Encyclopedia Britannica, 1952), vol. 38, p. 340.
13. *Twilight of the Idols,* Walter Kaufman ed. and tr. *The Portable Nietzsche* (New York: Penguin Books, 1982), pp. 499–500.
14. Rousas John Rushdoony, *Freud* (Phillipsburg, NJ: Presbyterian and Reformed, 1965) p. 12.
15. Ibid.
16. William Dannemeyer, *Shadow in the Land: Homosexuality in America* (San Francisco: Ignatius Press, 1989), p. 25.
17. Dr. Judith Reisman, and Edward W. Eichel, *Kinsey, Sex, and Fraud: The Indoctrination of a People* (LaFayette, LA: Huntington House, 1990).
18. Ronald Bayer, *Homosexuality and American Psychiatry: The Politics of Diagnosis* (New York: 1981).
19. Quoted in Dannemeyer, p. 39.
20. *Conservative Review,* February 1990. This article shows that child molestation is a common part of the homosexual lifestyle.
21. Ibid.
22. *AFA Journal,* June 1991.
23. *Christianity Today,* July 22, 1991.
24. Ibid.
25. *AFA Journal,* June 1991.
26. See William Dannemeyer, *Shadow in the Land: Homosexuality in America* (San Francisco: Ignatius Press, 1989), pp. 71–75.
27. *Washington Newsletter,* July 1991.
28. *Fort Lauderdale Sun-Sentinel,* September 6, 1991.

Chapter 3: The Firm Foundation

1. "To the highest authority."
2. G.K. Chesterton, *Charles Dickens* (London: Sheed and Ward, 1934), p. 27.
3. Cornelius Van Til, *The Defense of the Faith* (Phillipsburg, NJ: Presbyterian and Reformed, 1955), p. 8.

4. Greg Bahnsen, *Homosexuality: A Biblical View* (Grand Rapids, MI: Baker Book House, 1978), p. 28.

5. Jay Adams, *Competent to Counsel* (Phillipsburg, NJ: Presbyterian and Reformed, 1970), p. 139.

6. Greg Bahnsen, *Homosexuality: A Biblical View* (Grand Rapids, MI: Baker Book House, 1978), p. 82.

7. David Chilton, *Power in the Blood: A Christian Response to AIDS* (Brentwood, TN: Wolgemuth and Hyatt, 1987), p. 116.

Chapter 4: The True Tradition

1. "Lost arts."

2. G.K. Chesterton, *Charles Dickens* (London: Sheed and Ward, 1934), p. 47.

3. Quoted in, Martin Forbes, *History Lessons: The Importance of Cultural Memory,* (New York: Palamir Publications, 1981), p. 61.

4. *Rite Reasons: Studies In Worship,* December 1990.

5. *Church History,* February 1990.

6. Quoted in Tim Dowley, ed. *Eerdman's Handbook to the History of Christianity* (Grand Rapids, MI: Eerdman's Publishing Co., 1977), p. 2.

7. Ibid.

8. *Rite Reasons,* Ibid.

9. Quoted in Kendall S. Harmon, *Should Practicing Homosexual Persons be Ordained in the Episcopal Church Today?* (Shaker Heights, OH: Episcopalians United, 1991), p. 26.

10. *Journal of Religious Ethics,* 14/1, 1986.

11. Quoted in Cyril C. Richardson, ed., *Early Christian Fathers* (New York: Collier Books, 1970), pp. 337–338.

12. Peter Leithart, *The Promiscuous Society* (unpublished manuscript), p. 52.

13. Quoted in Lawrence L. Pouvre, *Canons and Councils* (London: Holy Trinity Evangelical Book Trust, 1967), p. 49.

14. R. J. Rushdoony, *The Institutes of Biblical Law* (Phillipsburg, NJ: Presbyterian and Reformed, 1973), p. 401.

15. See especially Deuteronomy 28.

16. Quoted in Reay Tannahill, *Sex in History* (New York: Stein and Day, 1980), p. 156.

17. Ibid.

18. Jaroslav Pelikan, ed., *Luther's Works* (Concordia Publishing House, 1961) Volume III, p. 255.
19. James Jordan, ed. *The Covenant Enforced: Sermons on Deuteronomy 27 and 28* (Tyler, TX: ICE, 1990), pp. 51–52.
20. *The Confession of Faith of the Presbyterian Church in the United States Together with the Larger Catechism and the Shorter Catechism* (Atlanta: John Knox Press, 1965), p. 232.
21. David Chilton, *Power in the Blood: A Christian Response to AIDS* (Brentwood, TN: Wolgemuth and Hyatt, 1987), pp. 81–82.
22. Ibid, p. 82. Emphasis added.
23. Alvin Plantinga and Nicholas Wolterstorff, ed. *Faith and Rationality: Reason and Belief in God* (Notre Dame: University of Notre Dame, 1983), pp. 222–223.
24. See Thomas Kuhn, *The Structure of Scientific Revolutions* (Chicago: University of Chicago Press, 1962).
25. There is however another way to defend the faith that is both rational and faithful. See Richard Pratt, *Every Thought Captive* (Phillipsburg, NJ: Presbyterian and Reformed, 1979); John Frame, *The Doctrine of the Knowledge of God* (Phillipsburg, NJ: Presbyterian and Reformed, 1987); and Cornelius Van Til, *The Defense of the Faith* (Phillipsburg, NJ: Presbyterian and Reformed, 1955).
26. *World,* September 14, 1991.
27. David Chilton, *Productive Christians in an Age of Guilt-Manipulators: A Biblical Response to Ronald J. Sider* (Tyler, TX: ICE, 1981), p. 383.
28. William Dannemeyer, *Shadow in the Land: Homosexuality in America* (San Francisco: Ignatius, 1989), pp. 113–114.
29. Ibid, p. 114.
30. Ibid, pp. 114, 116–117.
31. Ibid, p. 115.
32. *Cornerstone,* Volume 19, Issue 94.
33. *Church History,* February 1990.

Chapter 5: How Should We Then Live?

1. "Now or never."
2. G.K. Chesterton, *Charles Dickens* (London: Sheed and Ward, 1934), p. 39.

3. John Bunyan, *Pilgrim's Progress,* ed. Roger Sharrock, (New York: Penguin Press, 1965), p. 51.

4. *The Confession of Faith of the Presbyterian Church in the United States Together with the Larger Catechism and the Shorter Catechism* (Atlanta: John Knox Press, 1965), pp. 121–122.

5. Ibid, p. 126.

6. John Calvin, *Institutes of the Christian Religion,* 4:17:10 (Philadelphia: The Westminster Press, 1960), p. 1370.

7. *Modern Reformation,* July/August 1991.

8. Jay Adams, *Handbook of Church Discipline* (Grand Rapids, MI: Zondervan, 1986), p. 95. Quoted in Ibid.

9. Ibid.

10. John Frame, *Evangelical Reunion: Denominations and the Body of Christ* (Grand Rapids, MI: Baker Book House, 1991), p. 47.

11. Ibid.

12. David Chilton, *Power in the Blood: A Christian Response to AIDS* (Brentwood, TN: Wolgemuth and Hyatt, 1987), p. 194. On pp. 194–196, Chilton briefly lists examples of seven examples of Church ministries to the AIDS infected.

13. Gary DeMar, *Ruler of the Nations: Biblical Principles for Government* (Ft. Worth, TX: Dominion Press, 1987), p. 185. DeMar quotes *The Third Wave* (New York: William Morrow, 1980), p. 212.

14. William Dannemeyer, *Shadow in the Land: Homosexuality in America* (San Francisco: Ignatius Press, 1989), p. 159.

15. Weldon M. Hardenbrook, *Missing From Action: Vanishing Manhood in America* (Nashville, TN: Thomas Nelson, 1987).

16. To prevent any misunderstanding, we should state plainly that just because the Bible does not recognize the civil right to practice homosexual copulation does not mean that homosexuals do not have any civil rights at all. They have the same civil rights as anyone else—such as the right to a fair trial. The Bible prohibits the development of a police state by commanding rulers not to violate the laws of Christ.

17. *The Confession of Faith of the Presbyterian Church in the United States Together with the Larger Catechism and the Shorter Catechism,* (Atlanta: John Knox Press, 1965), p. 232.

18. Francis A. Schaeffer, *Two Contents, Two Realities* (Downers Grove, IL: InterVarsity Press, 1972.

19. David Chilton, *Paradise Restored: A Biblical Theology of Dominion* (Tyler, TX: Dominion Press, 1985), p. 215.

20. Ibid, p. 216. In context, Chilton is referring to legalized abortion.

Conclusion: Lance's Reprise

1. "By faith and assurance."
2. G.K. Chesterton, *Charles Dickens*, (London: Sheed and Ward, 1934), p. 24.

ABOUT THE AUTHORS

G EORGE GRANT has been active in efforts to renew and restore the Church for nearly two decades. He is a popular speaker and the prolific author of more than a dozen books on social policy, economics, history, and theology. Formerly Vice President of Coral Ridge Ministries, he now serves as Executive Director of Legacy Communcations. He lives in Franklin, Tennessee, with his wife, Karen, and their three children. He is currently at work on a novel and a series of biographies.

MARK HORNE is a writer and researcher who serves as contributing editor for Legacy Communications. His intellectual analysis of current societal trends has made him a significant new voice for renewal and restoration in the Church. This is his first book. He lives in Franklin, Tennessee, with his wife, Jennifer, where he is currently at work on several widely varying writing projects.